W9-AQS-816

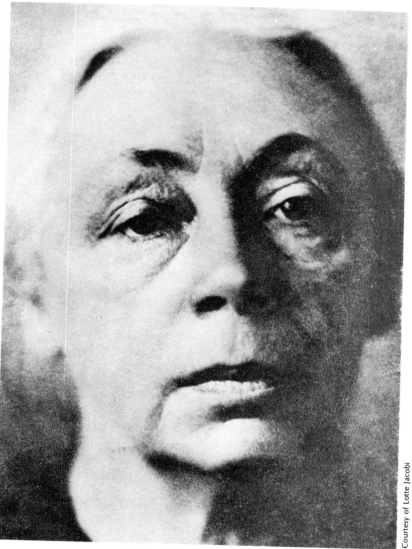

# Käthe Kollwitz: Woman and Artist

*By Martha Kearns*

⊏THE FEMINIST
⊐PRESS

ISBN: 0-912670-15-0
Library of Congress Catalogue Card Number: 76-6764

Art Director/Designer: Susan Trowbridge

This book was typeset in Journal Roman and Optima
by Automated Composition Services Inc., Lancaster,
Pennsylvania, with Mistral heads supplied by Nassau
Typographers, Plainview, New York. It was printed on
Perkins & Squier 60# Old Forge Opaque by Capital
City Press, Montpelier, Vermont.

The photographs used to create the montage
on the cover of this book are courtesy of the
Akademie der Künste, Käthe-Kollwitz-Archiv,
West Berlin, of Lotte Jacobi, and of Max Jacoby.
The montage was executed by Ruth Adam.

THE FEMINIST PRESS
dedicates this book
to the
Women's International League
for Peace and Freedom,
founded April 29, 1915.

"At such moments,
when I know I am working
with an international
society opposed to war,
I am filled with a warm
sense of contentment."

—Käthe Kollwitz,
*Diary and Letters*

AUTHOR'S DEDICATION

To women and their
revolutionary potential
to create a new world.

# CONTENTS

# LIST OF PLATES

# CHRONOLOGY
## of Major Events

| | |
|---|---|
| JULY 8, 1867 | Käthe Ida Schmidt born, Königsberg, East Prussia, to Katharina (née Rupp) Schmidt and Karl Schmidt |
| 1881–1882 | Begins art lessons with Rudolf Mauer, copper engraver |
| 1884 | Becomes engaged to Karl Kollwitz |
| MARCH 18, 1885 | Arrives in Berlin to study art under Karl Stauffer-Bern at Women's School of Art |
| 1888–1889 | Studies painting under Ludwig Herterich at Women's School of Art in Munich; learns etching in non-university classes |
| JUNE 13, 1891 | Marries Dr. Karl Kollwitz; moves to 25 Weissenburgerstrasse at Wörther Platz, northeast Berlin |
| MAY 14, 1892 | Gives birth to first child, a son, Hans |
| FEBRUARY 28, 1893 | Attends premiere of *Die Weber* [The Weavers] by Gerhart Hauptmann |
| FEBRÚARY 6, 1896 | Gives birth to second son, Peter |
| 1898 | Completes *Ein Weberaufstand* [Revolt of the Weavers] |
| 1899 | Receives gold medal for *Revolt of the Weavers* |
| 1902–1908 | Creates *Bauernkrieg* [The Peasant War] series |
| 1903–1911 | Begins series of freelance drawings on life of working-class families for *Simplizissimus* |
| 1904 | Visits Paris; attends sculpture classes at Julien Academy; visits Rodin; adopts Georg Gretor |
| 1907 | Awarded Villa Romana Prize; year's residence in Florence; takes walking tour from Florence to Rome |

| | |
|---|---|
| OCTOBER 23, 1914 | Son Peter killed at Dixmuiden, Flanders |
| 1917 | Fiftieth birthday retrospective show, Paul Cassirer Gallery, Berlin |
| 1919 | First woman elected to Prussian Academy of the Arts |
| 1922-1923 | Creates *Krieg* [War] |
| 1925 | Creates *Proletariat* [The Proletariat] |
| 1926 | Helps to found GEDOK, Gesellschaft der Künsterinnen und Kunstfreunde (Society for Women Artists and Friends of Art) |
| 1927 | Sixtieth birthday retrospective; visits the Soviet Union as guest of the government |
| JULY 30, 1932 | Places memorial sculptures *Die Mutter* [The Mother] and *Der Vater* [The Father] at Roggevelde Cemetery, Belgium |
| 1933 | Resigns from Prussian Academy under Nazi pressure |
| 1934-1935 | Creates the series *Tod* [Death] |
| JULY 19, 1940 | Death of Karl Kollwitz |
| JANUARY, 1942 | Last graphic, *Saatfrüchte sollen nicht vermahlen werden* [Seed for the planting must not be ground] |
| OCTOBER, 1942 | Grandson Peter killed in Russia |
| 1943 | Last self-portrait; evacuates to Nordhausen; on November 23, her home is destroyed by bombs |
| 1944 | Evacuates to Moritzburg, near Dresden |
| APRIL 22, 1945 | Dies at Moritzburg, at age seventy-eight |

# PREFACE

Although Käthe Kollwitz is one of the most well-known women artists in the Western world, this biography was necessary, for no account of her life had been written from a contemporary female perspective.

Three works, all written by women, were the most useful in researching her life. Kollwitz herself kept a diary and wrote many letters, and these writings provided the most valuable resource. In the course of my work a friend visiting Berlin read the original manuscript of Kollwitz' diary—in the Akademie der Künste—and selected passages from it; and this material, some of it printed here for the first time in English, was immensely helpful. *Sechzig Jahre Freundschaft mit Käthe Kollwitz* [*Sixty Years of Friendship with Käthe Kollwitz*] by Beate Bonus-Jeep, her best friend, gave an intimate memoir of their relationship and contributed vital information. And Muriel Rukeyser's poem *Käthe Kollwitz*, reprinted here, offered through its psychological insights a fine appreciation of the woman and the artist.

Readers unfamiliar with German may be disconcerted by variations in the spellings of proper names. The text of this book employs the *umlaut* (Käthe, Königsberg), while the English version of Kollwitz' *Diary and Letters* uses the Anglesized vowel form (Kaethe, Koenigsberg), and both forms appear in other sources quoted. Readers may also find discrepancies between titles of Kollwitz' graphic works as given here and as offered in other sources. My source for titles in both German and English is Otto Nagel's *Käthe Kollwitz*.

Chapters 1 and 2 of this book closely follow the two autobiographical essays that introduce Kollwitz' *Diary and Letters*, as these are the only reliable sources for her earliest years. Some episodes in the book are reconstructions of experiences in Kollwitz' life, dramatized because of their importance to her. With a few exceptions (notably, the opening scenes of Chapters 6 and 7, which, in both cases, had occurred a few years earlier), the chronological sequence of experiences, events, and works has been preserved as far as possible.

# ACKNOWLEDGMENTS

Some rare photos, prints, and drawings have been reproduced here alongside more familiar works. For the use of these little-known works I would especially like to thank Margaret Gaughan Klitzke, as well as Ruth Lehrer, Curator, and Kathie Hunt, Assistant Curator, of the Alverthorpe Gallery. For the rare photos of the artist, I am grateful to Lotte Jacobi, photographer, and Ilse Brauer, Käthe-Kollwitz-Archiv, Akademie der Künste, West Berlin. I am also indebted to the following persons for their help: Max Jacoby for photographs; Carl Zigrosser for the use of former manuscript files; Mina C. and H. Arthur Klein, Werner Timm, and Arne Kollwitz for copyright permissions; Arlene Raven, Selma Waldman, Karen Honeycutt, Meg Harlam, Karen Petersen, J. J. Wilson, Louis Kampf, Meo H.-Rentsel, and very particularly Milton Muelder for their time, thoughtfulness, and advice. The contributions of the following persons were also vital: Peter Buttenwieser, Gäby Stöckle, Lilian Evans, Lucy Queeney, Käthe Ostwald, and especially Rick Spaid.

On behalf of The Feminist Press I would like to thank Muriel Rukeyser for her elegant poem *Käthe Kollwitz*, reprinted here as an epilogue.

This book came into being through the vision, enthusiasm, and hard work of everyone at The Feminist Press, especially that of two sisters, Verne Moberg and Sue Davidson. I will always be grateful to Verne for her patience, encouragement, and support in the "early" and "middle" days of the manuscript. To Sue I give my deepest appreciation for the great energy, editorial skill, wisdom, and humor that she brought to the work; credit for the transformation of manuscript into book goes to her.

Finally, I am thankful for the togetherness of Sharon, Linda, Gale, Judith, Ellen, and most importantly Margaret, without whom this book would never have been written.

# 1

# My love for my mother was tender and solicitous.

*Katharina Schmidt lay resting* on the bed, exhausted from hours of labor in the close summer heat. It was July 8, 1867. The baby, born moments ago, suckled at her breast. The mother looked down at the child cradled in the warm curve of her arms and breathed a sigh of relief.

She was thankful that labor was over and that the newborn was a girl. She had given birth to three boys—two of whom had not survived—and now, her second girl. Pulling the soft blanket up to the top of the baby's tiny back she closed her eyes.

Karl, the father, was also happy that their fifth child was a girl, knowing that girls had better chances of surviving the early days of life than boys. He glanced at a photo of his wife proudly holding Julius, their first child. The boy they had called "the firstborn child, the holy child" had died shortly after birth.[1] Karl left Katharina sleeping and went to inspect the nursery, made ready for the baby. Like the rest of the house, this room was modestly furnished with family antiques, furniture that he had made himself, and pictures by the old masters competently copied by his wife.

Katharina and Karl Schmidt named their new baby Käthe Ida and soon gave her an affectionate nickname—Katuschen, or little Käthe.* The infant grew into a "quiet, shy . . . nervous" child,[2] who nevertheless delighted in the games and compan-

*Pronounced "Káy-teh"*

1

ionship of other children. The house in which she spent her first years was at 9 Weidendamm, in the middle of the East Prussian industrial city of Königsberg. The property fronted on the busy Pregel River, where "the flat brick barges docked and the bricks were unloaded in the yard."[3] Among these bricks and other construction materials used by her father's building firm, Käthe played out fantastic adventures with her older sister Julie, her older brother Konrad, and the neighboring children.

"Playing house" in the brick-piles was among the more sedate of their games.

> There were endless places to play and numerous adventures to be had in those yards. For example, a pile of coal had been unloaded from a boat and dumped in the yard in such a way that it sloped up gently and then fell off sharply on the side facing our garden. It was a risky matter to climb up almost to the brink. I myself never dared, but Konrad did. Another boy who tried it was hurt. . . .

> Then there was the pit filled with unslaked lime, with only a single plank across it. If you fell in, it was said, your eyes would be burned out.

> Then there were the piles of clay we used to build forts out of—one on either side of the yard. The attacking party threw balls of clay which could really hurt.[4]

Käthe was usually the youngest in the neighborhood gang, and although on the whole her companions treated her fairly, they also found it easy to bully her. "I was still very timid. I could not hold my own against the older children."[5] A high-strung child, she kept her feelings well hidden.

Birthdays were very special days of the year for Käthe, but her ninth birthday was a painful one.

> First of all, I did not like the number nine. Then I received a set of skittles [ninepins—nine wooden pins that are bowled at] as one of my birthday presents. In the afternoon, when all of the children were playing skittles, they would not let me play—I don't know why. As a result, I had one of my usual

> stomach aches. These stomach aches were a surrogate for all physical and mental pains. . . . I went around in misery for days at a time, my face yellow, and often lay belly down on a chair because that made me feel better. My mother knew that my stomach aches concealed small sorrows, and at such times she would let me snuggle close to her.[6]

In general, though, her mother was not physically affectionate toward any of her children. Käthe regretted her reserve, and therefore especially enjoyed the rare closeness with her mother. Except for a few instances, fixed in her memory because of their emotional intensity, Käthe could remember nothing specific about her mother when she was very young. Katharina Schmidt was always busy as a mother and wife, devoting her life to raising Käthe, Konrad, Julie, and the youngest, Lise—born three years after Käthe—and caring for her husband, Karl. "She was there, and that was good. We children grew up in the atmosphere she created."[7] The atmosphere was secure and loving, despite Katharina's undemonstrativeness.

One family incident revealed much about her mother's reserved, stoic character. The newest baby, Benjamin, had just turned one, and

> we were sitting at table and Mother was just ladling the soup—when the old nurse wrenched open the door and called out loudly, "He's throwing up again, he's throwing up again." Mother stood rigid for a moment and then went on ladling. I felt very keenly her agitation and her determination not to cry before all of us, for I could sense distinctly how she was suffering.[8]

Shortly after this incident, Benjamin died of meningitis, as had the Schmidts' firstborn son, Julius. Käthe desperately wanted to comfort her mother—"I loved her terribly"[9]—but could not, for Katharina's stiffness put her off. Her mother always remained aloof, with "that distant look of hers."[10]

Deeply touched by Katharina's suffering and by her unwillingness to show it, Käthe was also troubled by childhood fears of losing her mother. "In those days my love for my mother was tender and solicitous."

3

> I was always afraid she would come to some harm.
> If she were bathing, even if it were only in the tub,
> I feared she might drown. Once I stood at the win-
> dow watching for Mother to come back, for it was
> time. . . . I felt the oppressive fear in my heart that
> she might get lost and never find her way back to
> us. Then I became afraid that Mother might go
> mad.[11]

Yet Käthe never saw her mother break down. Without self-pity, without seeking to cast blame, she endured the loss of three of the seven children she had borne. "But although she never surrendered to the deep sorrow of those early days of her marriage, it must have been her years of suffering that gave her forever after the remote air of a madonna."[12]

While Katharina Schmidt never cried, tenderhearted, nervous young Käthe did, often and violently; some of her roaring and kicking tantrums lasted for hours.

> This stubborn bawling of mine was dreaded by
> everyone. I could bawl so loudly that no one
> could stand it. There must have been one occasion
> when I did it at night, because I remember that the
> night watchman came to see what was the matter.
> When Mother took me anywhere, she was thankful
> if the fit did not come over me in the street, for
> then I would stop dead in my tracks and nothing
> could persuade me to move on. If the fit came
> over me at home, my parents would shut me up
> alone in a room until I had bawled myself to ex-
> haustion. We were never spanked.[13]

Perhaps Käthe's childhood fits were unconscious expressions of her mother's pent-up rage and grief. But in later years, Katharina Schmidt's stoicism appeared in Käthe herself—and in many of her images of mothers.

As the daughter of a nonconformist religious leader who had suffered much political abuse, Katharina Rupp Schmidt had been raised to be religiously, politically, and socially broad-minded; she was a socialist who wanted to give her daughters as many opportunities as possible. Katharina's strict religious training helped to form her daughter's moral character: the child was unusually sincere and serious.

4

Katharina also possessed artistic interests and talents, indicated by the successful copies of the old masters with which she decorated her home. If artistic talent is transmitted by genes, perhaps it can be said that Käthe inherited some of her gift from her mother.

Katharina Schmidt had read Shakespeare, Byron, and Shelley in the original English—an uncommon achievement for an East Prussian woman of her day. But Käthe rarely saw her absorbed in reading and never heard her discuss what she had read. Neither did Katharina share her own experiences; thus Käthe learned little about her mother directly. Their primary communication was nonverbal. Katherina spoke through her emotional strength: that was her legacy.

Until Käthe was seven or eight, she paid scant attention to little Lise, three years her junior. Gradually, however, without being conscious of how it came about, the two sisters became "part of one another."

We were so merged that we no longer needed to speak in order to communicate with one another. We were really an inseparable pair. What we called "our game" could be played only with one another. We had no dolls, nor did we have any desire for them. But at the stationery store (Fraulein Sander's on Koenigstrasse) we used to buy sheets of theatrical paper dolls, all of them characters out of different plays. We colored these figures with water-colors and cut them out. There were over a hundred of them, and we played constantly with them. In our room we were our own masters; we played all over the room, turning tables and chairs upside down according to the inspiration of the moment. Greek mythology, Schiller's dramas, our own inventions— we were never at a loss for subjects. Building blocks were brought up, palaces erected, altars, sacrifices, *The Minstrel's Curse* enacted. . . . We were indefatigable. Lise, although she was three years younger than I, kept right up with me in everything and obeyed my orders. Without her, play was impossible.[14]

Käthe also liked to watch a neighbor make plaster casts. She often stood in the chalky atmosphere of his studio as he molded plaster, fascinated by the shapes of the thickening, yet pliant powdery liquid.

Like most children, Käthe was captivated by animals, especially horses. Her father stabled bays for the family and sometimes for his work, for he was a stonemason who built houses. His horses sometimes pulled construction materials from the yards to his building sites. For a while, he also kept a family carriage and a uniformed driver. But Käthe was less interested in the fancy carriage than she was in her father's brick wagons which, to her, were always associated with the streets of Königsberg. "They always moved in a procession at the slowest possible speed, dusty, groaning, squeaking, pulled by wretched nags and driven by coarse, crude drovers."[15]

When Käthe was nine, shortly after that very unhappy birthday, the Schmidts moved into a home her father had built on Königstrasse, one of Königsberg's newest and most fashionable streets. Käthe preferred the old neighborhood to the new one which was more middle class and which was far from those beloved construction yards where the children had once staged their reckless exploits.

If Käthe had lost some childish joy in the move to their new home, however, she gained a world of pleasure in the summer expeditions to the Schmidts' newly rented "peasant house" in Rauschen, a tiny fishing village on the Baltic Coast.

> There was no railroad; we rode in a *journalière*, which was a large covered wagon with four or five rows of seats. The rear seats were taken out and the back stuffed with all the things we would need for a stay of many weeks: bedding, clothing, baskets, boxes of books and cases of wine. What a joy it was when the *journalière* drew up in front of our house and all the things were loaded aboard. Then Mother, the servants, and we children (Father usually came later) would be stowed away on the front seats, and the driver would jump up to his special seat up front. The three or sometimes four horses would start, and off we would go. . . . Shortly before we reached Sassau we would catch sight of the sea for

the first time. Then we would all stand on tiptoe and shout: "The sea, the sea!" Never again could the sea—not even the Ligurian Sea or the North Sea—be to me what the Baltic Sea at Samland was. The inexpressible splendor of the sunsets seen from the high coastline; the emotion when we saw it again for the first time, ran down the sea-slope, tore off our shoes and stockings and felt once again the cool sand underfoot; the metallic slapping of the waves—that was the Baltic to us![16]

The Schmidts eventually bought the house at Rauschen, and the family returned there regularly. The free and active summers at the shore, which were the beginning of Käthe's love of the sea and of all the outdoors, were among the many advantages provided by her parents.

Käthe's father was a man unusual for his time and place, and, to a certain degree, for any time. Educated in the law, he had not followed his profession because his political, social, and moral views made it impossible for him to serve the authoritarian Prussian state. He disagreed with the right-wing politics of Joseph Radowitz, a top government official, and with the commanding military general, Prince Otto von Bismarck. Bismarck had recently achieved the unification of the several German states under the rule of a new empire dominated by Prussia. He had accomplished this feat by waging and winning the Seven Weeks War with Austria (1866) and the Franco-Prussian War (1870–71), in which France was forced to surrender Alsace-Lorraine, and the German-French border was defined. Germany's hegemony over Europe was thereby established for the next three decades.

Discouraged with the political climate of Bismarck's Prussia, Karl Schmidt became intrigued by the ideas of Karl Marx. Marx's message of socialist revolution had resulted in an abortive, premature revolt of Berlin workers in 1848, a few months after his views were printed in a pamphlet entitled *The Worker's Declaration of Independence (Communist Manifesto)*, which quickly became one of the most popular pieces of writing of its day. Its readable, historical analysis of the bourgeoisie and the proletariat gave many workers their first real hope of changing the inhuman conditions inflicted upon them as a result of too-rapid industrialization. Although the 1848 revolutionaries had been wantonly slaughtered by the palace guard, the spirit of socialism had not died. The socialist conviction that the proletariat were destined to overtake the bourgeoisie, the vision of international friendship among workers, had captured the imagination and devotion of many— among them, Karl Schmidt. Schmidt had joined the German Social Democratic Workers Party (the SPD) with religious fervor, focusing his faith on socialist ideology rather than on a spiritual deity. Having joined the SPD, he knew it would be moral and political suicide to attempt to practice law in right-wing Prussia. He turned to the art of stonemasonry and in time became an expert housebuilder.

Schmidt was a man of the future in his educational as well as his political views. Unlike many Prussian fathers—the model authoritarian patriarchs—the head of the Schmidt family was not a strict disciplinarian and he did not believe in corporal punishment. A moral idealist, he taught his children to correct their behavior through self-control, choosing to guide rather than force their development.

Karl Schmidt disapproved of the public schools, so the children learned in private schools and also at home under his guidance. In a day when girls were rarely encouraged to aspire to roles other than those of wife and mother, he personally helped to develop the individual talents of each of his three daughters, especially Käthe and Lise. He worked with his hands and encouraged his children to follow suit; he did not share the usual bourgeois contempt for manual work or for those who did it.

> At that period we already had the set of blocks that Father had made for us. They were big, solid blocks and we used them a great deal for building. We also had many long strips of wastepaper from Father's architectural designs. These were given us for drawing. . . . Father kept an eye on our work and soon began saving the strips of paper we had scribbled on.[17]

Soon it became obvious to the Schmidt family that Konrad was interested in drama and that Käthe and Lise were gifted at drawing.

Käthe liked to daydream almost as much as she liked to draw, and at about this time she became interested in love.

Her first crush was Otto Kunzemüller, the boy upstairs. Käthe and Otto would clamber over the next door fence or sneak down the cellar steps together, unwatched, whereupon one would bestow a highly solemn kiss upon the other. The recipient, first giggling, then reverent, would promptly return it. They called this "a refreshment."[18]

> I literally loved Otto so deeply that my whole being was filled to the brim. But since I was wholly ignorant in matters of love, and he, I imagine, no less so, the refreshment kiss was as far as we went. He made up the most fantastic cock-and-bull stories about his past life, and I believed them all. . . .
>
> One time Otto said to me that he could not marry me. Why? I asked in alarm. Because I belonged to the Free Congregation and he did not, he said. For my part, I had a bitter struggle over the question of marrying him because he had the awful name of Kunzemueller. Worse yet, the other boys always called him Kumstemueller.[19]

Käthe and Otto "played marvelously together,"[20] often outdoors with Otto's boyfriends—sledding, skating, playing ball. Käthe enjoyed being the only girl in this male company: "I was in their good graces in those days because I was good at ball-playing."[21] Then one day, unexpectedly, Otto moved away. Their love was ended. Käthe took it hard. She scratched an "O" into her left wrist.

> After this first crush of mine I was always in love. It was a chronic condition; sometimes it was only a gentle undertone to my ordinary life, and sometimes it took stronger hold of me. I was not particularly discriminating about my love-objects. Sometimes I fell in love with women. Rarely did the person I was in love with have the slightest suspicion of my feelings. At the same time I was plunged into those states of longing for I knew not what which torment the child at puberty.[22]

(text continued on page 12)

PLATE 1. Käthe Ida Schmidt.

PLATE 2. Katharina Rupp Schmidt and Karl Schmidt.

Like many preteenagers of her day, Käthe was greatly confused by the almost untouchable cloak of silence that fell over the topics of sex, love, and reproduction. Her parents didn't enlighten her. She went to her mother daily during this time—deliberately, timidly, trying to share feelings and questions.

> I needed to confide in my mother, to confess to her. Since I could not conceive of lying to my mother, or even of being disobedient, I decided to give my mother a daily report on what I had done and felt that day. I imagined that her sharing the knowledge would be a help to me. But she said nothing at all, and so I too soon fell silent.[23]

Unfortunately, these daily visits only made Käthe feel "the lack of any real friendship with my mother more distinctly than ever before."[24] Because of this silence on sex-related topics, Käthe continued for many years to feel ignorant and guilty about her own sexuality.

Her mother's puritanical attitude had been fostered by her own father's strict moral teachings. Julius Rupp was an idealistic, intellectual, and highly moral preacher who had been imprisoned thirty years earlier because his religious views had differed from those of Friedrich Wilhelm IV. Upon release, after two years of imprisonment, Rupp had founded a religious community called the Friends of Light, or the Free Congregation, based on the tenets of the early Christian communities. In spite of police and governmental assays to obstruct and persecute Prussia's first nonconformist religious community, the group survived for about a decade, practicing its ideals of education, labor, and communal property, and using the familiar form of address.

Now the Free Congregation held Sunday morning services for children and adults. Julius Rupp's sermons to the congregation were erudite and lengthy. Perhaps in reaction to her grandfather's scholarly approach to religion, Käthe "did not love God—He was far too remote. . . . it was Jesus I loved."[25] The children's class included

> discussion of the sermon, discussion of the Gospels, examination of a significant poem or longer poetic

12

work (such as Lessing's *Nathan the Wise*), and a bit of religious history. For the latter Grandfather had charts drawn up showing cross-sections of time.[26]

Though her grandfather's erudition intimidated her, Käthe liked his spirit, and while she was growing up, she respected him more than any other adult; he "was always ready to give, was always kindly and informative, and often laconically humorous."[27] The young artist noted his physical appearance more than his thoughts. She would remember him as

> tall, thin, dressed in black up to his chin, his eyeglasses having a faintly bluish tinge, his blind eye covered by a somewhat more opaque glass. Grandfather's hands were very beautiful; my mother's hands took after his. They were large and expressive in shape; he wore a signet ring.[28]

Later, a characteristic of Käthe's pictures would be the beautiful hands of many of her subjects.

If the Sunday morning service was painfully formal to Käthe, the hour after the service was often the most pleasant of the week.

> By the wide window stood two old armchairs facing one another. There my grandparents sat. The entire window was wreathed around by ivy. Usually the company talked about the sermon, but politics or any other interesting matters were also discussed. The atmosphere, since it was no longer wholly spiritual, was more comfortable for me. . . . Lise and I sat looking at the portfolio of pictures [a large collection of copper engravings which her grandfather had compiled]. Quiet as mice, we half listened to the conversation, but were more absorbed in the pictures. . . .
>
> This after-sermon hour in my grandparents' warm, bright room has stamped them in my memory as infinitely friendly, kind and intellectual.[29]

Five older women also figured prominently in Käthe's childhood. One of these was Aunt Berta, an unmarried aunt of Käthe's mother, who, like most "spinsters" of her day, had remained in the bosom of the family. She had made herself useful by teaching English and French to Käthe's mother and the other female Rupps. When Käthe knew Aunt Berta, she still lived "two stories up in my grandparents' house, in a sweet, old-fashioned room" in which Käthe and Lise delighted to visit her.

> Her room had the pleasantest old furniture, including a sofa with side arms which actually had drawers. She owned a complete Goethe in the small Cotta original edition; a plaster cast of the Amazon group in front of the National gallery; and a Goethe with Gellini's illustrations. Also, even in summer she always had some *Pfeffernuesse* [cookies rolled in powdered sugar] left over from Christmas. She first taught Lise and me to sew . . . and we always had a great deal to talk about with her. She was a wise old spinster, such as children are often very fond of. . . .[30]

The other older women who "contributed to rearing and shaping us" were more unusual than Aunt Berta—independent, unconventional, strong in their views.

> These were the Ulrich sisters and the Castell sisters. The Ulrich sisters were two aged canonesses. . . . Lonny Ulrich . . . had a face that was like Socrates' in its ugliness. We seldom saw her when she did not have some knitting in her hands. She was extraordinarily shrewd and intellectually keen. . . .
>
> . . . Later on, during the theoretic disputations between the followers of orthodox Rupp doctrine and my father's reformed doctrines, she vigorously opposed my father. . . . She had a peculiar way of weaving into her stories of personal experiences all sorts of reflections, logical deductions, moralisms. . . .
>
> Her sister Olga Ulrich (who by the way was not a member of the Congregation) lived in a canonry nearby and was the queerest old canoness imaginable. She had the keen wit of her sister Lonny, but with her it took the form of broad humor. She . . . was a kind of bohemian in the canonry. Often she went on long walking tours through Samland. She

constantly violated the rules of the order. If the chapter house were already closed, she would let her late visitors go out through the window.[31]

Unlike the Ulrich sisters, the Castell sisters, Henriette ("Yetta") and Ernestine ("Aunt Tina"), had a high seriousness unrelieved by verbal wit. The Castells were women who carried weight within the Free Congregation, and Yetta had also attracted notice in the larger world. She

> was a favorite figure in the humor sheets which attacked the Free Congregation during the period of reaction. . . . A fanatic nature enthusiast, she scorned all kinds of conventional and civilized behavior and often walked barefoot about the city.[32]

A poignant legend about Yetta made a lasting impression upon Käthe.

> Once [Yetta] decided to visit Goethe's Bettina von Arnim in Berlin. The difficulties of such a journey in the days before the railroad were enormous. But she *wanted* to visit Bettina. . . . She reached Berlin and went straight to Bettina's home. In her simplicity she was convinced that Bettina would instantly recognize her as a spiritual comrade and take her to her heart. Instead, a servant girl opened the door and said that her ladyship was not receiving. Whereupon Henriette turned about and set off for Koenigsberg that same day.[33]

Both Yetta and Ernestine were old women by the time Käthe and Lise came to know them. Ernestine was the only surviving member of the original Free Congregation who still clung to the sect's aspirations to emulate the simplicity of the primitive Christian communities. Käthe regarded her as an imposing person, one whom "nothing had been able to break or bend."

> She lived in an isolated one-story cottage situated on a road lined with old willows. . . . She had an injured leg that had never healed properly, so that the only way we ever saw her was sitting in her armchair, the bad leg in a horizontal position. . . .

*15*

> ... She still seemed to live in a different world from the real world. She knew Klopstock's entire *Messiah* by heart, and I have heard her recite long passages from it. ... She would not tolerate any realists, and above all not those who leaned toward materialism. Such persons seemed to crush her into silence, and she turned them away.[34]

Visiting their unorthodox "aunts" was only one of the diversions Käthe and Lise enjoyed. Another favorite pastime was wandering through the winding streets of Königsberg, unchaperoned.

> One thing for which I shall always be very grateful to my parents is the fact that they allowed Lise and me to wander about the town for hours in the afternoons. ... Their one stipulation was that we should not take walks in Koenigsgarten. ... However, we could cross through [Koenigsgarten] if our way led in that direction—and we usually saw to it that it did. In our own way we were a pair of highly conceited young chits; we let our scarves wave in the wind, dressed up, and were often silly and extremely childish.[35]

Having satisfied themselves by conquering Königsgarten, they were content to resume their meandering about town. They sauntered down to the shore of the Pregel River, past the medieval stone castle, past the tall Catholic cathedral, and on to their favorite haunt—the docks of the fruit and vegetable barges and grain ships. Here the dockhands or *Jimkes* worked, heaving crates, pulling ropes, and shouting directions. Usually the *Jimkes* were dressed in layers of sheepskin, hard leather, wool, and cotton; sometimes they wore rags.

Käthe was entranced by their strong bodies, their facial expressions, their sure, basic movements. They were "Russians or Lithuanians, good-natured people," who were fun-loving, entertaining, and cheerful; evenings, "they stayed aboard their flat, shallow ships, playing the accordion and dancing."[36] Käthe spent many hours watching them. Their hard-worked bodies, their plain, ageless clothes, but most of all, their lined faces held a mysterious beauty for her. They possessed a grandness of presence, manner, and movement that she had seen in no others and that she wanted to see again and again. They at once stimulated and satisfied her young aesthetic eye.

> All this apparently aimless loafing undoubtedly contributed to my artistic growth. For a long period my later work dealt with the world of the workers, and it can all be traced back to these casual expeditions through the busy commercial city teeming with work.[37]

## NOTES

1 Kaethe Kollwitz, *The Diary and Letters of Kaethe Kollwitz*, ed. Hans Kollwitz, trans. Richard and Clara Winston (Chicago: Henry Regnery Company, 1955), p. 18.
2 *Ibid.*, p. 17.
3 *Ibid.*, p. 15.
4 *Ibid.*, p. 16.
5 *Ibid.*
6 *Ibid.*, p. 17.
7 *Ibid.*, p. 18.
8 *Ibid.*, p. 19.
9 *Ibid.*, p. 20.
10 *Ibid.*
11 *Ibid.*
12 *Ibid.*, p. 18.
13 *Ibid.*, p. 17.
14 *Ibid.*, p. 25.
15 *Ibid.*, p. 18.
16 *Ibid.*, pp. 26–27.
17 *Ibid.*, p. 18.
18 *Ibid.*, p. 22.
19 *Ibid.* Literally, "Come along, Miller!"
20 *Ibid.*
21 *Ibid.*
22 *Ibid.*
23 *Ibid.*, p. 23.
24 *Ibid.*, p. 22.
25 *Ibid.*, p. 163.
26 *Ibid.*, p. 31.
27 *Ibid.*
28 *Ibid.*, p. 29.
29 *Ibid.*, p. 30.
30 *Ibid.*, p. 33.
31 *Ibid.*, p. 34.
32 *Ibid.*
33 *Ibid.*, pp. 34–35.
34 *Ibid.*, pp. 35–36.
35 *Ibid.*, pp. 27–28.
36 *Ibid.*, p. 28.
37 *Ibid.*

# 2

## I was keenly ambitious.

*Käthe hung the "Verboten" sign* on the door and walked back into the library. Lise took her place on the wide window-box seat. Turning her head to the left, toward Käthe, she sat very still. Her older sister quietly assembled a pencil, a thin black crayon, and a large piece of white scrap paper. She sat down on the floor and studied Lise's features for a long time. Then she began to draw. She lightly outlined the face, hair, neck, and shoulder lines; sketched in the eyes, nose, and mouth; and measured the face proportions against her thumb.

The eleven-year-old drew with intense concentration—first squinting up at Lise, then down at her drawing to create, end, or erase a line, then eyeing Lise again before returning to the paper for another look. The drawing captured her sister's small, broad forehead, high cheekbones, and large, oval face with its strong Slavic character. Young eyes looked directly out from the page. Filling in the details, Käthe drew with quick, sure motions of her wrist and fingers, shadowing the eyes, nose, mouth, and hairline. She squinted her left eye and held the drawing at arm's length for scrutiny. Lise's eyes were like hers: soft and kind.

Finished, Käthe stretched her arms and legs, while Lise, released from her pose, did the same. Käthe stepped back from the drawing and measured it from the perspective of a few feet. There were many errors, but good lines and shading predominated. Lise's eyes, particularly, were treated with skill and delicacy.

She took the drawing to her father, who expressed his satisfaction with it. After Käthe had run off to play, he opened a drawer labeled "Käthe's Work," to tuck it away. Before doing so, he removed from the top of the pile a drawing Käthe had recently completed, a large, ambitious composition called *Luther verbrennt die Bannbulle* [Luther Burns the Bull of Excommunication]. Influenced by her father's love of classical painting, Käthe was totally immersed in the concept of "high art"; as a result, she had depicted one of the major events of German and religious history—Luther burning the Pope's edict in public, denouncing all ties with Roman Catholicism.[1] Käthe's father recalled the family's pride and amazement at the drawing, especially their admiration of the heads of the common people in the crowd, whose features were those of *Jimkes*, expressing varying degrees of astonishment, fear, and suspicion.

Clearly their middle daughter, Katuschen, was gifted at drawing. Both Katharina and he encouraged her; he did especially, for he had dreams that Käthe would someday be a successful painter. In his opinion she would "not be much distracted by love affairs," since he felt she was "not a pretty girl."[2] Therefore, he planned to give her as much professional training in art as possible, though it was "unfortunate" that Käthe wasn't a boy, for her career, as a female, would be much more difficult. Even so, he was willing to support her training in art—which few fathers did in that day.

Complimented by her father's interest, Käthe worked diligently to please him. But her father's (and soon, her own) overwhelming ambition created a dilemma that would torment her for years.

Lise, who also drew, and very well at that, was as gifted as Käthe, if not more so. Käthe was jealous of Lise's talent as well as the attention she received for it. At the same time, she loved Lise "deeply" and, it is evident, possessively. She "had resolved never to marry; but Lise too was not to marry. She would stay with me all the time and belong to me, so to speak."[3]

One day, by accident, Käthe overheard her father say "something that bothered me for a long time afterwards."

20

> He had been astonished by one of Lise's drawings, and said to Mother: "Lise will soon be catching up to Kaethe."

> When I heard this I felt envy and jealousy for probably the first time in my life. I loved Lise dearly. We were very close to one another and I was happy to see her progress up to the point where I began; but everything in me protested against her going beyond that point. I always had to be ahead of her.[4]

Her ambition changed her relationship with Lise from one of complete love, companionship, and trust to one compounded with envy and rivalry. She did not want to compete with Lise, but she did not want Lise to replace her as the family artist, either. The threat of Lise's ability created in Käthe a single-mindedness that inspired her to ask for drawing lessons before Lise might think of asking.

> I had a clear aim and direction. In addition, of course, there was the fact that I was three years older than she. Therefore my talent came to light sooner than hers and my father, who was not yet disappointed in us, was only too happy to open opportunities for me. If Lise had been harder and more egotistic than she was, she would unquestionably have prevailed on Father to let her also have thorough training in the arts.[5]

Lise, however, was self-sacrificing, even to a fault. According to her sister, she was "infinitely goodhearted and easily hurt,"[6] gentle, and so unselfish that she did not ask for art lessons for herself. "I was keenly ambitious and Lise was not. I wanted to [become an artist] and Lise did not."[7]

Käthe took advantage of Lise's good nature and used her as a model—the best teacher, besides discipline, a young artist can have.

> I owe a great deal to Lise because she would sit as model for me, and never tired of it. When I was drawing and could not solve a particular problem, she would put herself into the pose; she was always a good model and endlessly patient.[8]

*21*

Not all of Käthe's developing intellect was concentrated on drawing. She detested the girls' academy that she attended but enjoyed the history and literature taught there. More important, her parents gave her as well as their other children the opportunity to develop themselves "without their pushing our noses into things."[9]   They opened up their library, where Käthe discovered the English painter William Hogarth and the German writers Johann Wolfgang von Goethe, Johann von Schiller, Heinrich von Kleist, Gotthold Lessing, Heinrich Heine, and Ferdinand Freiligrath. Goethe quickly became her favorite poet. She especially like his early lyrical poems praising the rational and irrational sides of nature as essentially good, powerful, and unknowable.

Her left-wing parents, however, favored popular naturalistic verse. Her father helped his children to appreciate poetry by reading poems. One of his favorite works was Freiligrath's translation of "The Song of the Shirt." At this time, in the 1870s, this poem, written by the English poet Thomas Hood, was translated into many languages and reprinted in newspapers in order to expose the inhumane conditions of factory workers.

> With fingers weary and worn,
>    With eyelids heavy and red,
> A woman sat in unwomanly rags,
>    Plying her needle and thread—
>    Stitch! Stitch! Stitch!
> In poverty, hunger, and dirt
>    And still with a voice of dolorous pitch
>    She sang the "Song of the Shirt"!
>
> Work—work—work—
> Till the brain begins to swim,
>    Work—work—work
> Till the eyes are heavy and dim!
> Seam, and gusset, and band,
>    And band, and gusset, and seam,
> Till over the buttons I fall asleep
>    And sew them on in dream![10]

Once as her father read the last lines, he became so moved that his voice grew fainter and fainter until he was unable to finish. His silent identification with the poor seamstress filled the room. In the silence Käthe, too, experienced the sweat, heat, and grind of a shirt factory and the working woman's numb fatigue.

Käthe was moved deeply by another poem by Freiligrath, "The Dead to the Living," in which the voices of the March Dead summon all survivors of that revolution to arm against capitalist profiteers and decadent monarchs. Thirty years before, on March 18, 1848, the Kaiser's militia had killed two hundred laborers who, inspired by a French uprising a month earlier and by the recently published *Communist Manifesto*, were protesting unjust working conditions outside the Kaiser's palace in Berlin. Like her family, Käthe identified with the two hundred March Dead martyrs. The poem "The Dead to the Living"

> made an indelible impression upon me. Battles on the barricades, with Father and Konrad taking part and myself loading their rifles—these were some of my fantasies of heroism at this time.[11]

Not all of Käthe's dreams were heroic, however. She sometimes suffered from nightmares, and sometimes a frightening hallucination recurred.

> I am lying in my bed in the semidarkness of the nursery. In the next room Mother is sitting in the chair under the hanging lamp, reading. I can see only her back through the half-open door. In one corner of the nursery lies a large coil of rope such as is used on ships. The rope begins to stretch out and unroll, silently filling the whole room. I want to call Mother and cannot. The grey cable blots out everything.[12]

Another recurrent nightmare theme was the sensation of a state of weightlessness. She had "the feeling I was in an airless room, or that I was sinking or vanishing away."[13] This weightless falling into space commonly represents a feeling of powerlessness, a fear of failure.

"There was a horrible state I fell into when objects would begin to grow smaller. It was bad enough when they grew larger, but when they grew smaller it was horrifying."[14]

When these visions fully terrified her, she would cry out, twitching frantically.

These states of mine alarmed my parents; they feared epilepsy. My parents would send Konrad to call for me at school because they were afraid I might have a seizure during the day, but this never happened. Both Konrad and I hated this arrangement. Instead of walking with me, he stayed on the opposite side of the street.[15]

Chronologically, the nightmare seizures were the third and last in a series of ailments that plagued Käthe's childhood and youth, the two previous ones having been crying tantrums and severe stomach aches. When any one of these disorders was a frequent visitor, she became self-conscious and depressed. The depressions lasted for hours, even days. "When in these moods I could not bring myself to use words to communicate with others. The more I saw what a burden I was being to the family, the harder it became for me to emerge from my mood."[16]

Now, at puberty, she was experiencing intense emotional and sexual feelings, yet she knew nothing about her own sexuality and nothing about intercourse or reproduction. The sexual fears arising from her ignorance undoubtedly contributed to her nightmares. Further, the attraction she felt toward women may have complicated and confused her sexual identity. This was a subject she could discuss with no one. Perhaps her father's ambition for her to become an artist, rather than a wife and mother, heightened her ambiguity concerning her sexual identity.

It is probable that her father's ambition for her roused other anxieties, for although he planned that she should become a great painter, Käthe had no role models, no examples of other successful women artists to follow. (Rosa Bonheur and Mary Cassatt were prominent in France but were as yet unknown to her.) How would she do it? Was it possible, or was it just an idealistic dream of her father? Would she *not* marry, in accord with her father's plans? If that were the case, would she continue to live with her parents, as most unmarried women did? Suppose that she were to combine marriage and a career—would the advent of motherhood force her to abandon her work, as was the case with virtually all women in such circumstances?

24

She had no answers to these questions. She was only very anxious, and she reacted physically, in convulsive fits, and, subconsciously, in nightmares of powerlessness.

It is often true that artists who express themselves visually—painters, sculptors, graphic artists—find it difficult, often impossible, to communicate the visual message in words. Some simply can't do it; many don't even try. Käthe's ailments probably expressed her frustrations at living in a stranger's land where, as yet, no one spoke her language; indeed, she herself didn't yet know all the idioms of her own tongue.

At the age of fourteen she began to learn them.

In the summer of 1881 Käthe began art lessons with Rudolf Mauer, a copper engraver with a large, second-floor studio in Königsberg's warehouse district. Mauer had been hand-picked by her father as one of the best teachers in Königsberg for Käthe's first art instruction.

Her first tools were a pencil, thin sticks of charcoal, dark-colored drawing crayons, ink, pen, and paper. Her beginning lessons were typical of the late-nineteenth-century's standard art classes for any talented beginner; the approach had not varied since the Renaissance. Formal training in art consisted in the student's proceeding "from copying from drawings and engravings, to drawing from casts of famous works of sculpture, to drawing from the living model."[17] Käthe and the two other girls in the class made drawings from plaster casts and models and copied drawings by the old masters. The hot, plastery clamminess of the studio mixed with the summer city air, hanging over them as they worked. She listened appreciatively to the "rhythmic tramping of men laying paving stones"[18] in the street below, a toil accompanying her own.

Into this fruitful period came Lisebeth and Karl Kollwitz and Hans Weiss, Konrad's friend. Lisebeth and Karl were orphans who lived with a family in Königsberg. Hans and Karl were Konrad's pals, and Lisebeth, Käthe and Lise's; but soon the Kollwitzes became friends of all the Schmidts, including Katharina and Karl. Lisebeth's personality was much gayer and lighter than either Käthe or Lise's; rambling around Königsberg became twice as much fun, with Lisebeth along.

Lisebeth's brother, Karl, was as cheerful as she, but older and inclined to politics; already he, Hans, and Konrad had accepted the premises of the Social Democratic Party as their own. The official policy of the SPD, "not a man nor a farthing for this system,"[19] meant that SPD representatives in the Reichstag would refuse to vote for any budget that would "tax the workers and peasants to sustain the tyranny of the capitalist state, and maintain the courts, policy, and army of the rulers."[20]

At first the sophisticated discussions of the three young men disconcerted Käthe, but they fascinated her and she listened intently. As she became acquainted with their political jargon, she began to participate with animation. Much of the talk centered on August Bebel, cofounder of the SPD, and his feminist views. Bebel's pioneering work, *Woman and Socialism*, had been published just a few years before, in 1879, and had already caused a great stir through Germany. According to Bebel, it was the goal of socialists

> not only to achieve equality of men and women under the present social order, which constitutes the sole aim of the bourgeois women's movement, but to go far beyond this and to remove all barriers that make one human being dependent upon another, which includes the dependence of one sex upon another.[21]

He predicted the dissolution of marriage, believing that socialism would free women from their second-class status: "In the new society women will be entirely independent, both socially and economically."[22] And it was his view that society would become more humane as women rose from their slave caste: "The development of our social life. . . demands the release of woman from her narrow sphere of domestic life, and her full participation in public life and the missions of civilization."[23]

Käthe took Bebel's thoughts seriously and debated his views with Karl, Konrad, and Hans. Hans was fanatical and overbearing, impatient with the views of others; Karl, on the other hand, valued Käthe's opinions and thoughts. She found her discussions with Karl—about socialism, art, medicine, free love, marriage, and revolution—rewarding. She liked his kind and unassuming manner very much, and soon their separate views and dreams of the world became interwoven.

Between the opposite natures of Hans and Karl stood Konrad, whose passion at this time was theater, not politics. He wrote and directed plays, which were performed by the family. Konrad's romantic tragedies and Karl's poetry readings entertained the Schmidts, their relatives, and friends.

Käthe enjoyed performing in Konrad's plays, although the pretentious speeches sometimes bored her. Awaiting her cue in the makeshift "backstage," she occupied herself with the placements of objects onstage, studying the changing scenes as they juxtaposed old and new objects to frame yet another visual, dramatic, and emotional dimension. Her instinct for the dramatic was undoubtedly developed further by this casual participation in Konrad's plays.

Käthe later made clear, in her journals, the debt she felt she owed to her home environment. In her view, it was a "blessed atmosphere" for a child, pervaded by "a fruitful and meaningful tranquillity."[24] The Schmidts were middle class, intellectual, and highly serious in their religious and political beliefs. They were not an artistic family in the strict sense, but they were progressive; and Käthe's development owed much to the broadness of their views.

Historically, women had most commonly become artists as daughters or nieces of prominent, successful artists. If the female members were taught the family profession—as some were—they might carry on the family reputation through their own work. While women did in some cases become artists without this sort of entrée, this happened rarely.

Although Karl Schmidt was not an artist, he was a skilled craftsman. His high regard for technique, his steady encouragement, and his financial support made it possible for Käthe to receive the best art training then available to a female. Moreover, in her home environment the three disciplines of poetry, politics, and theater lent their cast to her imaginative and serious eye.

At sixteen, Käthe was old enough to enter Königsberg's Academy of Art, where she wanted to study. It was here that she first encountered institutionalized discrimination: being

(text continued on page 30)

PLATE 3. *Selbstbildnis, lachen* [Self-portrait, laughing] , 1885, drawing.

*28*

PLATE 4. Käthe Ida Schmidt.

female, she could not be admitted to the academy. Fortunately, her father understood the crucial importance of training to a young artist, and so he enrolled her in studies with a fairly well-known painter in Königsberg, Emile Neide. "I therefore took private lessons with Neide, along with a young girl from Tilsit."[25]

Neide painted naturalistic scenes from the world of crime (some of which Käthe considered "pure kitsch"). He enjoyed a small reputation as the painter of one powerful canvas, *Weary of Life*. As a student in the Wilhelm-Dietz School in Munich—the best art school in Bavaria at that time—Neide had concentrated on the dynamic naturalism of the French painter Gustave Courbet. Neide did not initiate painting styles, ideas, or techniques, but he knew his trade expertly and competently interpreted the tenets of naturalism to Käthe.

In 1883, under Neide's instruction, she composed an illustration to Freiligrath's "The Emigrants," which laments:

> I cannot turn my eyes away,
> I must linger near and stare
> As your hurried hands pass all you own
> To the sailors standing there.[26]

This drawing portrayed the subjects, humble, newly arrived immigrants, resembling the *Jimkes* of Königsberg. Käthe's first composition showed great technical and dramatic skill, and it pleased both Neide and her father.

The following year, her seventeenth, brought many changes.

During that year, 1884, Käthe's grandfather died. While his age had taken a great toll, including partial blindness, he had continued to be actively involved in the lives of those around him, and his death was deeply felt.

Also in 1884 Karl Kollwitz, now a premedical student in Königsberg, made an engagement proposal to Käthe, and she accepted. While she was not in love with Karl, she found him compatible; and she did like him very much. More important, she knew that Karl loved and admired *her*.

Käthe's father, however, feared that this engagement would thwart his plans for Käthe's future as an artist. Understandably, he felt that marriage would inhibit her artistic career, and therefore he determined to send her away to art school. He wanted her to reconsider her engagement while continuing her studies.

In this same year, Käthe made an exciting and memorable journey.

> When I was seventeen, my mother made a trip for her health to a spa in Engadin. My father sent my younger sister Lise and me with her. Besides being a trip for the sake of Mother's health, this little vacation was intended to show us Berlin and Munich—especially Munich.[27]

They rode by coach and train to Berlin, where they stayed with the oldest sister, Julie, and her husband, Hofferichter. The young couple lived in Erkner, a Berlin suburb, where, by chance, Julie's husband had met Gerhart Hauptmann, a young poet and dramatist. Soon the two men had become fast friends and were entertaining each other often.

During their visit Hauptmann gave a dinner party for the painters Hugo Ernst Schmidt and Arno Holz, Julie and her husband, and Julie's family. Everyone wore festive rose wreaths and sat at a long dinner table decorated with yellow roses. Käthe was enchanted with this company of older artists, who were also socialists. They drank wine, as Hauptmann read from Shakespeare's *Julius Caesar*; and Käthe, like everyone else, was touched by the gay, carefree mood.

Hauptmann described Käthe at this party: "fresh as a rose in dew, a charming, clever girl, who, because of her extreme modesty, did not speak freely about her calling as an artist but let it be known by her sure, sensitive manner."[28] For Käthe, it was "an evening that left its mark. . . . a wonderful foretaste of the life which was gradually but irresistibly opening up for me."[29]

After their stay in Berlin the three rode south to Munich, whose art charmed Käthe completely; every day for a week she visited Munich's Pinakothek Museum. She was ecstatic upon seeing the voluptuous, dynamic paintings of Rubens.

> Rubens! I was carried away by Rubens. At the time I owned a small volume of Goethe. When the feeling completely overwhelmed me, I wrote in the margin

of the book: "Rubens! Rubens! The early poems of Goethe! 'The temple has been built for me....'" Goethe, Rubens, and the feeling I had about them formed one complete whole.[30]

She was reluctant to leave Munich until she saw the open stagecoach in which they were to travel to Engadin. A cushioned two-seater bench was perched high in the back; Käthe and Lise mounted a small ladder to reach it, while their mother seated herself in front. From their cushy, high seats, the sisters took in everything, shouting gleefully and singing songs to people and places along the way. Their mother, unable to resist their contagious joy, sang along in a rare, genuinely carefree, happy mood. "Mother at this time was only forty-seven, so beautiful and so gay."[31]

At St. Moritz Pass, Konrad joined them. Back from a visit to London, he was anxious to tell them the latest socialist news. Marx had just died. Konrad, who was acquainted with Marx's close friend and colleague, Friedrich Engels, had sat long into the night with Engels, discussing the future of socialism in the light of this recent event.

With Konrad along, the three begged their mother to take them to Italy. She at first adamantly refused, but as the trio continued to plead, she agreed that they might venture at least as far as the Italian border.

They transferred to a small cart, which creaked on to Maloggia Pass, accompanied by the spirited voices of Käthe and her family singing Slavic folksongs in the heady mountain air.

## NOTES

1 Otto Nagel, in colloboration with Sibylle Schallenberg-Nagel and Hans Kollwitz, *The Drawings of Käthe Kollwitz*, ed. Werner Timm (New York: Crown Publishers, Inc., 1972), p. 14.

2 Kollwitz, *Diary and Letters*, p. 23.

3 *Ibid.*, p. 26.

4 *Ibid.*, p. 24.

5 *Ibid.*

6 *Ibid.*, p. 26.

7 *Ibid.*, p. 24.

8 *Ibid.*, p. 26.

9 *Ibid.*, p. 25.

10 Thomas Hood, "The Song of the Shirt" in *Best Loved Poems*, ed. Leonard S. Davodow (Reading, Penn.: The Spencer Press, 1936), pp. 184–185.

11 Kollwitz, *Diary and Letters*, p. 25.

12 *Ibid.*, p. 21.

13 *Ibid.*

14 *Ibid.*

15 *Ibid.*

16 *Ibid.*, p. 18.

17 Linda Nochlin, "Why are There no Great Women Artists?" in *Woman in Sexist Society*, ed. Vivian Gornick and Barbara K. Moran (New York: Signet New American Library, 1971), p. 494.

18 Kollwitz, *Diary and Letters*, pp. 23–24.

19 Rosa Luxemburg, *Rosa Luxemburg Speaks*, ed. Mary-Alice Waters (New York: Pathfinder Press, 1970), p. 34.

20 *Ibid.*

21 August Bebel, *Woman and Socialism*, trans. Meta Stern (New York: Socialist Literature, 1910), p. 7.

22 *Ibid.*, p. 466.

23 *Ibid.*, p. 238.

24 Kollwitz, *Diary and Letters*, p. 36.

25 *Ibid.*, p. 37.

26 Otto Nagel, *Käthe Kollwitz* (Old Greenwich, Conn.: New York Graphic Society, 1971), p. 15.

27 Kollwitz, *Diary and Letters*, p. 38.

28 Adolf Heilborn, *Die Zeichner des Volks I: Käthe Kollwitz* (Berlin-Zehlendorf: Rembrandt Verlag, 1933), p. 36.

29 Kollwitz, *Diary and Letters*, p. 38.

30 *Ibid.*

31 *Ibid.*

# 3

## The free life
## of the artist allured me.

*Portfolio and luggage in hand*, Käthe stepped
onto the bustling train platform, her eyes searching the crowd
for Konrad. There he was, taller than she had remembered him.
In another moment they were embracing and exclaiming. Sharing small pieces of family news, laughing at their private jokes,
they made their way through the teeming Banhof.

In the street, Konrad's face sobered. He said to Käthe,
taking her by the arm, "There's one place I want to show you,
first off. You'll soon understand why."

Käthe's own round, young face grew serious, reflecting
his changed mood. She did not question him, but only nodded.
They set off past the horse-and-carriage taxis and the many
rag-wrapped vendors selling housewares, newspapers, vege-
tables, and fruits on the streets of Berlin. At last they stood
beneath an old stone arch carved with the name "Friedrich-
shain Cemetery."

Entering, they came upon line after line of square gray
stones. On some of them complete names were chiseled, only
the last on others, while on some there were no names at all.
All bore the inscription: "Died, March 18, 1848." Here lay
the March Dead martyrs, the nearly two hundred workers
slaughtered thirty-seven years ago, to the day, in the German
revolution of 1848.[1]

They were quite alone among the endless procession of
graves. They stood for a long while, wordlessly, then turned
back to the street.

Konrad had some good news. In spite of the "antisocialist laws" aimed specifically at the Social Democratic Party, the party had received two million votes in the last election. Since 1878, when the "antisocialist laws" had been enacted at Bismarck's behest, the publications and meetings of the SPD had been outlawed and, on occasion, brutally suppressed by the police. Yet many more workers were coming to agree that capitalism was responsible for the greed of employers, landlords, and government. Under the extensive organization of the SPD, many were now seeking to transform their capitalist economy into a socialist one so that workers could control the conditions and share equally in the profits of their labor.

While the German Social Democrats claimed the same revolutionary Marxist ideology as the Russian Bolshevists, they were, in practice, reformist. Thus, the SPD concentrated upon gaining parliamentary power to bring about socialist reforms within the capitalist system. This effort appeared to be bearing fruit. Despite the fact that the SPD was not one of the "approved" political parties of Germany, people were voting for its candidates, even electing them to the provincial and federal legislatures.

Konrad showed Käthe the University of Berlin, where he was studying economics, and his residence.

Although in 1885 women were not allowed to study alongside men in German art schools, the Berlin Academy of Art had by this time annexed a Women's School, which Käthe was to attend. The women's institution was consistently smaller in size, facilities, faculty, and curricula, as well as less prestigious than the larger Academy.

That night she settled in her first "home away from home," a small furnished room in a boardinghouse for women students near the university.

Käthe's first university professor, Swiss-born Karl Stauffer-Bern, was a jack-of-all-arts; at twenty-seven, he had already displayed talents as a poet, painter, sculptor, and etcher, and was a perceptive teacher as well. Stauffer-Bern had little respect for the sort of work favored by the Academy in 1885— enormous, academic canvases of battlefields. He apparently had not much more respect for his own work, which had brought him great success; he pronounced his admirers "blind." During this time he wrote to a friend that "among Berlin's one-and-a-half-million inhabitants, there isn't anyone of my own age who I feel is a kindred spirit in the world of art, so here I am, with no one to turn to for companionship, it's the very devil."[2]

Käthe herself fared better in finding companionship. At her first meeting with a sister student, Beate (or Emma) Jeep, the two became fast friends. Emma Jeep described her first impression of Käthe as a carefree young woman, "a barefooted girl from the mountains of Albania, who, without the aid of her hands, balances a water pitcher on her head and climbs easily to the well on the mountaintop; then, because she walks with great steadiness, climbs down the mountain without spilling a single drop."[3] Käthe was dressed simply, according to her own taste, in a tailored dress made of soft blue muslin.

From the beginning Emma and Käthe addressed each other by their last names, "Jeep" and "Schmidt," a practice they continued throughout their lives.

Eagerly Jeep and Schmidt shared their portfolios with one another. Then Käthe presented hers—consisting largely of anecdotes, and illustrations to poems—to Stauffer-Bern. At first he thought her work typical of her locale, for the subjects were Slavic and Russian peasants drawn in a realistic style. But when he saw *The Emigrants*, he exclaimed, "But this is just like a Klinger!"[4]

She had never heard of Max Klinger, Prussia's most skilled artist of the then-popular naturalism, a school of thought which deemed people to be predetermined victims in a bitter struggle for survival. As an art form, naturalism emphasized photolike images of actual persons, scenes, and conditions, often in the most minute, even microscopic detail. Unlike artists working in other styles, naturalist artists featured women as subjects as frequently as men. *The Emigrants* convinced Stauffer-Bern that Käthe could excel in the graphic arts of etching and lithography, requiring expert, subtle drawing skill, in which Klinger had perfected his naturalist techniques. Although Käthe objected when he urged her to follow in Klinger's path, "Stauffer-Bern's instruction was extremely valuable for my development. I wanted to paint, but he kept telling me to stick to drawing."[5]

Along with the other students, Käthe learned to copy the model in precise detail, line, and measured proportion. She drew from plaster models of parts of the female torso or the entire body. Or she drew bony, wrinkled old men, half-dressed, in formal pose, "who we were somehow supposed to make into beautiful paintings."[6] Women art students were not allowed to sketch from nude female models! At Käthe's request, though, Jeep often posed nude for her in the privacy of their rooms. Female models were introduced in Berlin life drawing classes in 1875, but women art students were not admitted to these until 1893, and even then the model had to be partially draped. Another "repressive regulation" of the Berlin Academy was that no pencils were allowed for drawing: only red and white chalk.[7]

In spite of this mechanistic regimen, however, Käthe absorbed the stimulating effects of Stauffer-Bern's teaching. At his suggestion she went to see Klinger's *Ein Leben* [A Life] at a Berlin exhibit. The life Klinger had drawn in these fifteen etchings was that of a young woman who had lost her virginity to her lover and who thus, in the eyes of the bourgeoisie, had "fallen" into unredeemable sin. The series reflected the double standard held against women at the turn of the twentieth century: females were prohibited from engaging in any pre- or extramarital sexual relations; and yet it was understood that, because of their naturally "seductive" sexual natures, women would engage in these activities nonetheless. Thus all women were believed to be helplessly "predestined" to fall into sexual temptation. In *A Life*, Klinger simultaneously mirrored and mocked this moral hypocrisy. One print, *Into the Gutter*, shows a young woman being shoved into an open sewer by a horde of grotesque, sadistically grinning figures. This extremely accomplished and powerful series stirred Käthe: "It was the first work of his I had seen, and it excited me tremendously."[8]

At the end of the school year she left Berlin with the assurance that Stauffer-Bern was interested in her work and would support her in pressing her father to let her attend art school again the following winter.[9]

*38*

Back home, my father persuaded me to paint a genre picture. I started *Before the Ball*, and at my father's urging I finished the painting, in spite of my inward impatience with it. The following year, while I was in Munich, Father had the painting framed and entered in an East Prussia traveling exhibit. The picture was bought, and the buyer ordered from Miss Schmidt of Koenigsberg, currently in Munich, a companion piece to be entitled *After the Ball*. This order was missent to an East Prussian Miss Schmidt whom I did not know; she happily accepted the commission, and I was not required to paint a sequel to *Before the Ball*—which also made me happy.[10]

Käthe helped her mother with household duties while she finished *Before the Ball*, whose theme, she felt, was "the worst trash."[11] She also returned to her former teacher, Neide, for drawing and especially painting lessons; for even though Stauffer-Bern had perceived her talent for the graphic arts, Käthe, influenced by her father's wish, dreamed of being a painter and so pursued as her major study the art of oils, colors, and painterly technique. At this time she was still planning to return to Stauffer-Bern when the shocking news reached her that he had gone mad and suddenly died in Italy.

Between lessons and chores she continued to see Karl; and at last, one day in 1889, she accepted his engagement ring. This simple act was shortly to produce major repercussions: "My father, who saw his plans endangered by this engagement, decided to send me away once more, this time to Munich instead of Berlin."[12]

The intellectual climate that Käthe entered in Munich in 1889 was sophisticated and challenging. Munich, like Paris, was the cultural and academic center of its country, and, unlike Berlin's, the Munich Academy of Art had been founded on high aesthetic principles and progressive, libertarian attitudes. The Academy's sense of high purpose and its relaxed learning environment undoubtedly helped to set the tone for Munich's art world and intellectual climate, which was highly receptive to the latest European art and thought.

Emile Zola's vivid, naturalistic novels exerted a great influence in this university world. The recent performance of Henrik Ibsen's *A Doll's House*, with its shocking message of women's emancipation from the bonds of bourgeois marriage, permanently changed the lives and expectations of many young women. August Bebel, too, in numerous public speeches, drew attention to capitalism's enslavement of women; in the analysis of contemporary society offered in his *Woman and Socialism*, Bebel pointed out that "marriage constitutes one phase of sex relations of bourgeois society; prostitution constitutes the other."[13]

The Academy shared its professors with the Woman's School of Art; and once again Käthe was fortunate enough to have a good teacher—Ludwig Herterich. Less insistent than Stauffer-Bern that Käthe should focus upon drawing, Herterich welcomed her into his painting class.[14]

Käthe went eagerly to her first studio class, on Türkenstrasse, in a large, bare room with a small, rectangular model's platform in the center. As her eyes followed the movements of the students in their long skirts, weaving gracefully among the solid shapes of easels, tables, stools, and chairs, she suddenly saw a familiar form. One of the students standing by an easel was Jeep!

Delighted by their reunion, Jeep and Schmidt chatted while they prepared for class. The studio buzzed noisily as students put on stiff cotton smocks, blotched with myriad colors, over ankle-length dresses, then scraped paint from canvases, cleaned them with turpentine, mixed colors, prepared their palettes, and balanced three-legged easels around the model's platform. Käthe liked their air of purpose.

In the midst of these busy preparations, Jeep caught sight of Schmidt's engagement ring. She was shocked and dismayed. Marriage was taboo to all the students. She understood, of course, that Käthe was not aware of this common stand. Loyally, she whispered a word of congratulation to Käthe, but her manner had become constrained; she absorbed herself in her palette. Meanwhile, the preclass din had dropped to a murmur of hushed conversation. Jeep knew that it would not be long before the students would be discussing Schmidt's engagement.

She was right. Word had spread quickly that a new student was engaged. The students were galled, confounded, and confused. Activity slowed as hostility stilled the room.

At last a student stood up to defend Käthe. Now Käthe realized that it was her engagement ring which had cut off Jeep's conversation and reduced everyone else to suspicious whispers or silence.

Celibacy was the first commandment of the art school.[15] The women art students considered marriage an act of betrayal, for it meant abandoning their artistic work. What value did the sacrifices, troubles, and expenses of the training have, they argued, if studying art was only a transitional stage between adolescence and marriage? They had exchanged many ideas about marriage, exploring the serious problems it presented and concluding that when a woman marries, her artistic work becomes second in importance to her husband.

The students agreed: all men wanted to marry a good housewife who would adjust to her husband's needs. It was impossible for a woman to be married *and* an artist. Even if the man were fortunate enough to earn a high salary, or wealthy enough to afford an extra housekeeper, the wife would still have to tend to house duties that would sap her time, desire, and energy for artistic work. They also understood that the free life of the student artist would be impossible to maintain after marriage.

As Jeep wrote about this classroom "trial" of her friend, years later, she remembered that Schmidt listened composedly to the discussion about her. Schmidt did not feel that the others were completely wrong. She herself had wrestled for a very long time with the question of marriage *and* art versus marriage *or* art, and had not found a solution. She did not respond to any of their opinions, because she had no reply. Also, she had resolved to remain silent on the subject until she had proved what she could do.[16] Yes, she was engaged, but she wasn't sure how much it would hinder her artistic work. She didn't know if she would be able to manage the two demanding roles of wife and artist, but she hoped to; and until and unless the two roles should prove unmanageable, Käthe was determined to commit herself to both, although it was her intention to dedicate the majority of her time to her work.

Her classmates, after a period of initiation, began to include her in their busy, exciting, and free way of life, both in and out of class. Käthe considered some of these women very gifted and was "delighted by the spirit of freedom which prevailed among [them]."[17] It was not long before she adopted her classmates' bohemian attitudes, dress, and behavior as her own.

Emulating the Munich students, who flatly rejected the dress-standards of their middle-class parents, Käthe quickly came to feel comfortable in her rough painting smock, which, never laundered, soon became an impermeable coat of color splots. One morning, according to Jeep, Käthe, being out of turpentine, left Herterich's class, without removing her painting smock or putting on a hat (the symbol of a proper bourgeois woman), and crossed the street to a hardware store. There she presented her empty clay container and asked that it be filled. This daring act, Jeep speculated, probably gave rise to the widespread rumor about the Academy that "in the morning the artists are already drunk, for they take stone bottles out with them then, and search the stores for even more hard liquor"![18]

Käthe felt she was learning a great deal about art. "Herterich knew how to train my eyes, and in Munich I really learned how to see."[19] However, she experienced some of her most beneficial art lessons outside of class. Herterich's teaching seemed "mannered" to her; his emphasis on color was not to her taste.[20] But the night sessions of the "Composition Club" gave her a chance to approach her work more independently, using her imagination on her own choice of subjects and models without worrying about being corrected or stifled by the teacher.

The informal Composition Club was composed of other women students together with three well-known artists—Otto Greiner, Alexander Oppler, and Gottlieb Elster. Members of the club hung their work on the walls of the Glückscafé [Good Luck Café], a small den where many Academy students gathered for *café au lait*. One night Greiner, a very talented and respected artist, particularly in drawing, came into the Glückscafé and, noticing new drawings, walked over to examine them. Seating himself on a bench, he slid along slowly, surveying the new work. At one of Käthe's drawings, he stopped. In admiration, surprised at its composition and beauty, he asked—of everyone, and of no one in particular—"Do all of your students draw so well?"[21]

It was the custom of the club's members to select a topic for their evening meetings. One night the Composition Club picked "Struggle"[22] as its drawing subject. Käthe had just read Zola's *Germinal*, a powerful novel about a strike of coal miners in northern France against their bosses; and from this she chose the scene in which two men, Lantier and Chaval, fight over a young woman, Catherine, in a smoke-filled tavern. In this shadowy drawing, titled *Germinal*, the two men, left center, are locked, off-balance, in a wrestling hold; at any moment it seems they will tumble to the floor. The peasant woman, Catherine, stands in the extreme right foreground, slightly bent over, one hand to her mouth as she watches in confusion and terror. Near the men a chair lies on its side. In the center background stands the tavernkeeper, barely silhouetted, in a white apron.

*Germinal* showed excellent perspective, composition, movement, and, though a bit dark, an understanding of light. Better than most student work, it received a great deal of praise from her colleagues. "For the first time I felt that my hopes were confirmed; I imagined a wonderful future and was so filled with thoughts of glory and happiness that I could not sleep all night."[23]

But another proposal for the future alarmed her. In a recent letter, her father had mentioned that Lise was drawing so well that he was considering sending her to study in Munich also. This news reactivated all of Käthe's dormant, unresolved feelings of jealousy toward Lise, as well as insecurity about herself. She felt an anxiety she had not experienced for years. The idea of Lise's coming to study unnerved her: What would she do if Lise turned out to be more skilled or more successful than she? She loved Lise—how unfair it was to be threatened by her! She didn't want Lise to surpass her; was it possible, then, that they could be equal, without her becoming jealous of Lise's achievements? Maybe. It was hard enough to be a young woman and an artist. Many of her classmates, who were very ambitious, were nevertheless disheartened, for a woman art student graduated to a limited number of opportunities for work or study And yet, she didn't want to discourage Lise's hopes. Käthe experienced "the most contradictory feelings: joy at the prospect of her coming and at the same time fear that her talent and personality would overshadow mine."[24] She hated these feelings but could not free herself from their hold on her.

There was not any immediate way to resolve her unwanted but genuine conflict with Lise. Käthe seems to have left the matter for time to resolve. She took up her work with fervor, curiosity, and love, and began the struggle for technical knowledge.

A new "Etching Club" had formed. Though photography and the still camera had grown more popular, celluloid film had not yet been invented. The photographic process was therefore still a cumbersome method of reproduction. Thus, the older arts of printing—copper engraving and especially etching—were being reassessed for their aesthetic and practical advantages. Like photographs, etchings could present a scene in detail, but they were more reliable than photographs and could be reproduced in countless editions, in black and white or color. Respected etchers and engravers formed the Etching Club to relearn, practice, and perfect these nearly forgotten arts and to invite students and artists in other media to attend their afternoon workshops.

Käthe readily accepted their invitation and paid the required fee. The club rented a large second-story loft near the Academy. Work tables, stools, chairs, double sinks, and presses filled the room. Stacks of chemicals, paper, and tools stood on the side shelves and tables. Small and large shiny, red copper plates, about a quarter of an inch thick, were shelved and ready for use. The side of the copper plate was not a straight edge but beveled so that the printed etching had a uniformly grooved, built-in frame.

Jeep also joined the Etching Club and learned the art alongside Käthe. She has left a detailed account of Käthe's first etching lesson, which reflects as much appreciation for the art as for the distinctive and disciplined artist her best friend was becoming.

Schmidt was given the tool, a sharply tipped, double-edged knife with a steel blade two inches long. She put her hand around the comfortable, sturdy wooden handle. . . . It was impossible for the etching knife to penetrate the copper, however, because the metal was too hard. First it had to be covered with wax.

The plate was picked up with tongs by the instructor. A small chunk of wax and some grainy asphalt were put on a tray, then placed over an oil lamp burner. After a few minutes, when the wax-asphalt had melted, it was poured onto the unused plate, then rubbed on to the plate with a chamois.

After a few minutes' rubbing the waxed plate was removed from the heat to let stand, and a thick, clear glaze hardened on the copper. As this careful preparation was shown, one had the sense that Schmidt had already acquired a passion for this medium.

The waxed surface had to be darkened in order for the etcher to distinguish lines, so the plate was again picked up with tongs, and quickly waved, wax side down, over snuffed candle smoke. This dyed the film black on contact. . . .

The coal-black plate was now ready for drawing, so Schmidt found an empty table to work. Her right hand gripped the etching knife surely as she pressed it into the black wax. The manner in which Schmidt etched was much freer and [more] expressive than what they were used to; her etching looked more like a pen-and-ink drawing. Gradually the copper lines showed the face of an old man. In the open space next to him she drew an anatomical study of the human ear. The copper face and ear shone out impressively from the blackened plate; she felt satisfied, and ready to etch.

Now she looked at the expert. "The etching procedure—give it to me," she said, and, laughing, wrote a few large letters in an open space, and gave it to him.

He put the plate in an appropriate sized bowl and poured the caustic etching acid onto it. The acid steamed up where the etching needle had gone through [the wax], making deeper lines in the copper plate. He then poured the acid back into its container, and the plate was held under running water until the acid was rinsed off.

Now Schmidt had to wash off the wax layer, and the plate was clear before her again, but with the etched drawing on it.

The plate was now rubbed with heavy black printing ink. Paper was placed carefully over the plate, then wooden rollers pressed over the paper and plate several times.

Schmidt was very excited and anxious about it, and, finally, the paper was given to her.

What was this now? The drawing on the blackened plate with copper shining through had looked impressive, but the result was a few lines on a piece of paper.

The expert made it clear to her that every etcher experiences this same disappointment at first. *Now* begins the work. Not for nothing is etching an old art of printing! He made her lay her print upside down, and put a mirror up to it so she could see it right side up as she worked. . . .

Schmidt continued to work industriously. Her style of secure and penetrating lines was already apparent. In this first etching, even though this medium had been unfamiliar to her, she succeeded in showing an old man, sitting in an overcoat, with strong, dark color tones, and a detail of the human ear.[25]

In this first lesson Käthe had learned that etching required manual dexterity and strength, intense mental concentration and patience—all of which she knew she had and was willing to give. She had also discovered that its lengthy, careful method suited her: her creative process was not one of instant inspiration but of arduous technical, emotional, and intellectual labor.

Student life was not all work. With the other students, Käthe took long walks in the nearby countryside and visited beer halls in the evenings.[26] She also enjoyed dressing up for masquerade balls—a pleasure she would favor throughout her life—and, with her own house key, she now felt free to follow her interests in and outside of Munich. One of her classmates gave her Danish writer Arne Garborg's *From a Man's World* to read, and this short novel, with its sound insights on the lives of women, made a deep impression on her. She also attended Bebel's lectures and read his book *Woman and Socialism*, a scathing critique of capitalism's oppression of women. With her reading of this work, Käthe now added a feminist perspective to her socialist one.

One of the artists she knew painted very poor genre paintings but excelled at mountain climbing, a sport she loved also. That year she climbed high into the Austrian Alps with him and another Alpine guide. She thought it great adventure to belay—to climb with ropes and cleats—especially when they climbed through a "chimney" miraculously formed by rocks, trees, brambles, and flowers, on the way to an awesome height. When she returned from this expedition, fulfilled and happy, she proudly reported the Alpine guide's praise: "this woman climbs like a nimble-footed goat!"[27] Käthe cherished this praise more than the *Pour le mérite* (a Prussian award for military valor!) she was to receive later for outstanding achievement in art.

At school, she continued to struggle with painting, but was aware of her deficient sense of color, especially when compared with that of her sister students Sommer, Slavona, and Geselschap. "Color was my stumblingblock."[28] Käthe did not perceive colors the way Herterich did, so she "used a trick to win a favored position in the class: I painted the way I knew he wanted me to paint."[29] It was at this time that she happened to read Klinger's brochure *Malerei und Zeichnung* [Painting and Drawing] which he had written three years earlier, in 1885. The reading of this technical but stimulating essay led to one of the major turning points in Käthe's career. The essay emphasized that

> Drawing has a freer relationship [than painting] to
> the representable world; it gives fantasy wider play

to imaginatively color and enhance the thing represented. . . . Line, the oldest element in the visual
arts, determines the whole form. . . . Moreover,
drawing in line invites one to cyclical compositions
. . . presenting the artist with a cornucopia of fantastic notions and images. . . . The draftsman,
however, looks perpetually at the unfilled holes,
the yearned-for and barely attainable. . . . The
painter bodies forth optimism, but the draftsman
cannot escape his more negative vision, beyond
appearance.[30]

Reading this, Käthe "suddenly saw that I was not a painter at
all."[31] This realization motivated her to seek more technical
know-how from the Etching Club, her sole source of education in the graphic arts. She experimented with additional,
more difficult etching methods, those that applied "aquatint"
and "soft ground" with varnish or sand to the regular etching
procedure. She strove to learn all she could, for although she
didn't want to leave, she feared that this spring term would
be her last.

Käthe began to have second thoughts about marriage:

I so liked the free life in Munich that I began to
wonder whether I had not made a mistake in bind-
ing myself by so early an engagement. The free life
of the artist allured me.[32]

She was loath to give up the intellectual stimulation of her
friends and Munich. But should she risk breaking her engagement? This conflict, too, she left to time to resolve.

Reluctant to conclude their independent life in Munich,
Jeep and Käthe, with another woman student, took a trip to
Venice. There they shared a room in a lodging house where
Käthe, after the first night, woke up to find herself scratching
bedbug bites. Unable to afford a glamorous gondola, they
rode the public launches from one end of the city to the other,
feeling free and easy and on their own. But soon they had to
travel to their separate homes.

Back in Königsberg, Käthe swapped tales of student adventures and plans for the future with Karl and Konrad. Their
mood was more optimistic than the last time the three of them

had met, for the new emperor, Kaiser Wilhelm II (grandson of the former Kaiser), had just repealed the "antisocialist laws" restricting the activities of the SPD. However, the repeal was motivated more by his dislike of Bismarck than by love for the SPD: Wilhelm II, too, was a bumptious militarist who tolerated no dissension in the ranks of the world's strongest military power.

Underground for more than a decade, the SPD now surfaced as an important legal and political force with significant representation in the Reichstag and in various provincial legislatures. Konrad, full of academic economic theory, planned to return to Berlin and the intense, growing leftist movement there. A socialist newspaper, *Vorwärts!* [Forward!] had just been organized, and Konrad was interested in writing articles for it about economics and theater.

Karl Kollwitz, meanwhile, was finishing his final year as a medical student, and had decided, probably because of Konrad's glowing accounts, to intern the next year in Berlin. Käthe was happy to be with Karl again, but when her father said that she might return to Munich if she wished to, she accepted the offer "gladly."[33]

Her father did not make the same offer to Lise, because Lise became engaged at this time and discontinued her studies in art. Käthe must have felt relieved, for now her deep fears about Lise, herself, and her work would no longer threaten her. She knew that Lise would devote her life to her husband, Georg Stern, and to their family, for it was her habit to deny herself for those she loved. In this case, the opinions of Käthe's classmates about the effects of marriage on a woman artist were vindicated, for Lise would never again devote herself seriously to art. Käthe, on the other hand, now wanted and needed to work daily at her art.

In Munich she lived again on Georgenstrasse, in the women students' boardinghouse. Her father had offered her only this one additional semester of study, although the choice of Munich over Berlin was her own. She reentered Herterich's school.

In this last semester, she turned again to drawing and to her most accessible subject—herself—in pen, pencil, charcoal, and wash. At seventeen, she had drawn a self-portrait,

*Selbstbildnis en face, lachend* [Self-portrait, laughing]. Unfinished, it reflects a carefree young woman, her round face radiating with her hearty laugh. Now, in 1889, she completed two successful self-portraits. In one of them, she is standing, looking at us sideways, with a steadfast, concentrated gaze, her full, closed lips, jaw, and chin set proudly in frank determination. Her right hand holds the lapels of her cloak in a gesture of authority that appears almost Napoleonic. In the other pen-and-wash drawing, *Selbstbildnis mit Studien Kollegin* [Self-portrait with Student Colleague], she sits in the foreground at a table with another student (probably Jeep, for her figure resembles the tall, willowy forms of Käthe's earliest nude studies of women). This study reveals a good painterly technique (building up composition, perspective, and light-dark sensitivity) plus her own very sharp, discerning eye. In 1889 she also drew Lise sitting and reading. It is clear from this portrait that Lise and Käthe looked remarkably alike, almost like twins, although Lise's features were finer and more delicate.

Aside from these studies Käthe produced nothing of value in her last term. She was very disappointed at the flatness of her final opportunity for studying art, and regretted that she had not chosen to go to Berlin where "there was a noisy ferment about life."[34] That winter she returned to Königsberg, dejected and at odds with herself, for she still wanted—and knew she needed—more professional training.

From the proceeds of the hateful genre paintings she had sold, she was able to rent a small studio, where applying herself to her work helped to fill the gap of needed lessons. She continued to draw herself, producing five good head studies. Four of these face forward, displaying varying degrees of emotional character and depth. One *Selbstbildnis nach halbrechts* [Self-portrait, from the Right Side], an extreme close-up, cut off at the hairline, reflects a candid, confident gaze, an aggressive, jutting chin, and a full, sensuous mouth. In another, the artist sits up stiffly, as if at military attention, looking at us proudly, even haughtily, with a bold, unflinching stare; one eye, nearly closed, conveys great passion. In a half-face study, her cupped right hand holds up her head, shielding some of her forehead as she looks penetratingly out at us, a pose she will repeat often. In the last self-portrait of 1891, Käthe looks sideways with an untroubled, tender expression; her jaw is firmly set.

A friend of hers, Helene Bloch, also had a studio in Königsberg, and with her Käthe discussed socialism and "the woman question," as everyone called it. The two women artists were impressed with the ideas of Karl Kautsky, the leading theoretician of the SPD, who favored reform rather than revolution. Bloch noted that "in Königsberg we had weekly get-togethers in my studio during which we read Kautsky's popularization of Marx's ideas."[35]

Käthe devoted the majority of her working time to painting, however. Though she had read Klinger's *Painting and Drawing*, in practicality she hadn't "yet completed the transition from painting to working in line." Her foremost desire was still to paint. "To be exact, I wanted to transfer the scene from *Germinal* to canvas."[36] In order to obtain the best models for this, she made morning sketches at sailors' taverns, where "visiting them at night was as much as one's life was worth."[37]

By this time she was able to draw with pen, pencil, chalk, and charcoal; paint with ink and wash, and etch; but she could not lift the same scene intact onto canvas. Try as she might to perfect her painterly technique in the same way that she had mastered drawing and etching, she found that she had no feel for color or its great and subtle uses; nor did color or nature inspire her in the same way as the lines and expressions of working people.

Early mornings, after breakfast, she walked a short distance through the snow to her studio, where she tried again to match the color before her eyes to that on the palette, brush, and canvas.

> I look out on a garden with trees, and in the morning the branches of the trees are white with frost, then later black as coal when the frost has melted off. I try both times of day, and it is very difficult to paint them correctly. Do you know, I find it quite good to work alone this winter. I believe that in this way one realizes how much talent one really possesses, and that one can find one's way.[38]

But each morning there appeared little or no progress from the day before. Her canvases showed some beauty and drama, were quite competent in themselves, but, next to her drawings, she knew that they appeared weak, muddy, and lacking in dramatic tension. She was beginning to admit that her sheer will, however strong, could not provide her, after two years of study, with the knack for color and painting.

Out of all her efforts with various art forms, it was the one struggle she lost.

## NOTES

1 Nagel, *Käthe Kollwitz*, p. 17.
2 *Ibid.*, p. 18.
3 Beate Bonus-Jeep, *Sechzig Jahre Freundschaft mit Käthe Kollwitz* (Berlin: Karl Rauch Verlag, 1948) p. 28.
4. Nagel, *Käthe Kollwitz*, p. 17.
5 Kollwitz, *Diary and Letters*, p. 39.
6 Bonus-Jeep, *Sechzig Jahre*, p. 19.
7 Nicholas Pevsner, *Academies of Art, Past and Present* (Cambridge: Cambridge University Press, 1940), p. 223.
8 Kollwitz, *Diary and Letters*, p. 39.
9 *Ibid.*
10 *Ibid.*
11 *Ibid.*
12 *Ibid.*
13 Bebel, *Woman*, p. 174.
14 Kollwitz, *Diary and Letters*, p. 39.
15 Bonus-Jeep, *Sechzig Jahre*, p. 33.
16 *Ibid.*
17 Kollwitz, *Diary and Letters*, p. 40.
18 Bonus-Jeep, *Sechzig Jahre*, p. 27.
19 Kollwitz, *Diary and Letters*, p. 40.
20 *Ibid.*
21 Bonus-Jeep, *Sechzig Jahre*, p. 27.
22 Kollwitz, *Diary and Letters*, p. 40.
23 *Ibid.*
24 *Ibid.*, p. 24.
25 Bonus-Jeep, *Sechzig Jahre*, pp. 37–42.
26 Kollwitz, *Diary and Letters*, p. 40.
27 Bonus-Jeep, *Sechzig Jahre*, p. 24.
28 Kollwitz, *Diary and Letters*, p. 40.
29 *Ibid.*
30 Max Klinger, *Malerie und Zeichnung* (Berlin: Inselbucherie, 1891), pp. 28, 37, 44.
31 Kollwitz, *Diary and Letters*, p.

40.

32 *Ibid.*

33 *Ibid.*

34 *Ibid.*, p. 41.

35 Käthe Kollwitz, *Briefe der Freundschaft und Begegnungen*, ed. Hans Kollwitz (München: List Verlag, 1966), p. 150.

36 Kollwitz, *Diary and Letters*, p. 41.

37 *Ibid.*

38 Bonus-Jeep, *Sechzig Jahre*, p. 44.

# 4

## I lived as a human being must.

*Karl had good news:* he had a position in Berlin! He had been one of the few young doctors chosen to implement a new plan of social and medical insurance for workers. Several years earlier, Bismarck had sought to undercut the Social Democratic Party's appeal by introducing the first European system of health insurance in which accident, sickness, and old age expenses of "the workers and their families" were covered by a *Krankenkasse*, a health insurance fund, raised from mandatory fees, in which the workers, their employers, and the state shared. Women received *Krankenkasse* benefits as dependents. Though now a doctor and a member of the professional class, Karl was a socialist. He did not simply want to make money; he was sincerely interested in serving people who were as poor as he had been as a young orphan.

Käthe was also pleased that Karl had a professional position that suited his politics, and, more important, that it was in Berlin. Karl was very excited about his prospects, and soon Käthe caught his enthusiasm. As they discussed the future they might build together, she thought back over the seven years of their engagement. There had been happiness and satisfaction; but there had also been fear, hesitation, and ambivalence.

In those seven years, it seems clear that she had, to some degree, internalized her classmates' belief that female artists must not marry: it was easy for her to observe that few married women *had* succeeded as artists. And she had enjoyed her freedom and independence as a single woman. Thus, she had swung back and forth between opposing forces.

She knew that, were she to stay at home, her father would probably support her, but she refused to put herself in that condition of dependency. She did not want to stay in Königsberg. She did not want to follow the example of her Aunt Lina who, in spite of her gifts as a singer, had abandoned her ambitions because her mother considered it improper for a woman to sing in public. The "days at home which were so leaden and boring" gave Käthe "the desire to get away, just to have things different and to live my own life. Just not to go on in the humdrum, traditional style."[1]

But in 1890, to leave home and live on one's own was far easier wished than done. There were virtually no opportunities for women artists in the business world. Even if Käthe had felt confidence in her one marketable skill—etching—her sex eliminated her from the job of newspaper illustrator, where this skill could be exercised; for the work entailed travel and irregular hours, conditions that made it "impossible" for a woman to fill the job. Except in Königsberg, where she would probably live with or near her family, Käthe, as a single woman, could look forward only to tight social restrictions and, in the matter of earning a living, long hours at low-paying, routine jobs. In spite of the great interest in "the woman question," she would eventually, if not immediately, find herself trapped, professionally and socially, if she tried to live independently as an artist.

On the other hand, if she married Karl, her independence would be greater than it was at home; as a wife in Berlin she could enjoy a more active intellectual and social life than she could as a single woman in Königsberg.

Karl's working as a *Kassenarzt*, or Health Insurance Doctor, certainly seemed a good way for him to earn a living for the family. But would she really have enough time and space to create—or would she be a slave to Karl, as her classmates had predicted? She was so stymied by this conflict that, finally, she made an arbitrary decision: yes, she would marry. She did not feel it was an easy or even a sound decision; it was a "leap in the dark."

> We were not building upon a firm foundation, or at
> least one firmly believed in. There were grave con-
> tradictions in my own feelings. In the end I acted
> on this impulse: jump in—you'll manage to swim.[2]

Her mother, reassured by the news, told Käthe, "You will never be without Karl's love."[3] Her mother must have been well aware that, regardless of talent or ambition, there was little future for a husbandless woman. If her artistic ambition or career should collapse, Käthe would always have Karl to love and provide for her, and, in turn, she would always have Karl to care for.

But her father feared the worst; for he knew how little time—if any—his daughter would have for creative work once she married and bore children. He was bitterly disappointed and dropped his hopes for Käthe's future as an artist.

> He had expected a much faster completion of my
> studies, and then exhibitions and success. Moreover,
> as I have mentioned, he was very skeptical about my
> intention to follow two careers, that of artist and
> wife. . . . Shortly before our marriage my father said
> to me, "You have made your choice now. You will
> scarcely be able to do both things. So be wholly
> what you have chosen to be."[4]

In all likelihood, Käthe's decision to marry was in part a rebellious act necessary for her emotional and artistic growth. She did not care to have her father involved in her art. Already he had forced her to paint "kitsch" genre paintings, entering them in various exhibits. He had exerted a great deal of pressure on her to be a painter, and a great one, and she appreciated this; but she could not be pushed. At school she had enjoyed a few minor successes, but at home she had always faced the difficulty of seeking both to please her father and to create work that expressed *her*. Her will to be an artist was still very strong, but her confidence in herself, particularly as a painter, was much too shaky for her to gamble her entire future on. She needed time to work, experiment, and grow in her art. Of all the choices available to her, marriage was the only one that could offer the unlimited time, the emotional and eco- nomic security that she needed to maintain her work.

57

In her refusal to accept her father's position that to be an artist she must remain unwed, Käthe was, ironically, mirroring the spirited character of the very man she now resisted. Her father had refused to accept Prussia's political system and had yet succeeded in life—as had her maternal grandfather, who had rejected the religious establishment of his day. Käthe, equipped with the same independent spirit, determined to continue her work in spite of the pressing demands made by marriage. Her father's attitude toward her marriage contributed to an unstated but observable drive to prove to him that she could be both an artist *and* a wife.

This independence of spirit, backed by an indomitable will, was an essential part of her artistic personality; without this toughness, she felt that she could not have accomplished her art. She referred to her own drive and strength as qualities that distinguished her, for example, from the more gifted but softer, more "feminine" Lise. Interestingly, however, it was not in such a context that she later discussed her "masculinity," but rather in the context of her early physical development.

> As I look back upon my life I must make one more remark upon this subject [her physical development]: although my leaning toward the male sex was dominant, I also felt frequently drawn toward my own sex—an inclination which I could not correctly interpret until much later on. As a matter of fact I believe that bisexuality is almost a necessary factor in artistic production; at any rate, the tinge of masculinity within me helped me in my work.[5]

As this passage indicates, Käthe made a connection between her early physical attraction to women and her later discovery, as an adult, of that trace of masculinity that she found almost essential to art. While apart from this passage, Kollwitz did not, in her writings, directly refer to the subject of her "bisexuality," its influence on her life and work can nevertheless be traced.

She identified her youthful love of women as "masculine." Later, as a student in Berlin, and especially in Munich, certain aspects of her personality set her apart from other women art students: the qualities of tenacity, self-confidence—even arrogance—ambitiousness, intellectual creativity. Whether these characteristics are "masculine" or not, she observed them in men more frequently than in women, and was aware of them in herself.

At the same time, she found that the best art demanded the full use of the "feminine" qualities of intuition and subjectivity, along with the more "masculine" use of intellect and objectivity. As she gradually came to appreciate this, she affirmed the artistic personality that contained "masculinity" (the ability to love women; intellectual strength) as well as "femininity" (emotional expressiveness, introspection). With this ability to affirm her "bisexuality" or complementary duality, she became a more mature and more powerful artist.

Her bisexuality evidently influenced her creative psyche more than it affected her sexuality. It is not known whether she ever acted on her feelings for women, whether she wanted to, or whether she would have been able to, considering her society's prohibitions and her own inhibitions. But her love for women enabled her to love herself—something essential to every artist. Even her early self-portraits project self-assurance. They are, at the same time, free of egotism or narcissism; they show the artist examining herself for the sake of understanding; they are frank studies of an imperfect, struggling, finite human. It is the same with her depiction of other women. She did not, with her "tinge of masculinity," absorb male bias against women; her portraits of working-class women show clearly that she appreciated women as whole human beings.

Thus her bisexuality, more spiritual than genital, did not alter Käthe's decision to marry, although it did affect the way she would live. Marriage places many women in a subservient role, determining the way they live for the rest of their lives; it is to Käthe's credit—and probably to that of her "masculinity"—that even within the confines of marriage, she valued herself *as an artist* above herself as a wife.

Karl knew this. For seven years he had waited patiently as she wrestled with the seeming incompatibility of marriage and art. From the first, she had made it clear that she would not give up her work if she married him. She loved Karl, but was not "in love" with him, as he was with her. Unlike most women of her time and place, Käthe always expressed more concern with her work than with her marriage. Karl, on the other hand, concentrated a very great deal of attention upon their relationship. This is not to say that there was a "role reversal" in their relationship. Karl was simply very devoted, kind, optimistic; Käthe was complex, introspective. Their marriage was more balanced than the typical patriarchal marriage of their day.

They planned to marry as soon as Karl found an apartment in Berlin. Käthe understood, of course, that an apartment large enough to accommodate a painter's studio was beyond their means. Out of necessity, then, she discarded her dreams of being a painter. Shortly before the wedding she wrote to a student friend, Paul Hey:

> In general, I draw now more than I paint. From the practical consideration, I will hardly have enough money to rent a studio in the first year of my marriage; in the cramped quarters which one lives in there, to paint oil paintings is a sad thought. For the first time in my life I have conceived of a large plan for a painting: the struggle scene from *Germinal*, which I had made as a charcoal sketch in Munich. I started it straitway, but am stopped. I can't paint the painting any more till spring, and in Berlin I can't pursue it because there will be no room. So I am making all the preparatory studies which I will need for it, and I etch everything so I will have as much practice in etching as possible.[6]

Karl found a tenement in a working-class section of North Berlin; they were now able to plan their wedding.

Prior to the event, some of Käthe's Munich classmates sent her a large etching of Joan of Arc, by a certain "Besnard," a French artist whom they all admired. To remind her of their student days, they chose the centuries-old symbol of the fighting strength and forced martyrdom of a lone woman.

A few weeks later, on June 13, 1891 (Karl's twenty-eighth birthday), Käthe and Karl were married. Käthe, twenty-four, felt a special warmth toward Karl; she took their marriage to heart, although the formal ceremony was of little importance to her.

The couple moved to an apartment on 25 Weissenburger-strasse, No. 58, on the corner of Wörther Platz, in North Berlin, now East Berlin. In 1891 Weissenburgerstrasse was a busy cobblestoned thoroughfare—"used daily by hundreds of commercial vehicles. The omnibus and horse traffic goes on until about 1:30 A.M."[7] This traffic, however, did not immediately bring many patients to Dr. Kollwitz' door. The young couple scrimped and saved, and "often stood at the window or on the tiny corner balcony, watching the passersby in the street below, hoping that one or other [sic] of them would find his way into the waiting-room."[8]

For the next fifty years they moved from floor to floor within this corner tenement. Three flights of dingy stairs led to their apartment. In the middle of their living room stood a big wooden table; over this hung a homemade lampshade, decorated with silhouettes. Standing lamps, straight and stuffed chairs, and a comfortable sleeping couch upholstered in a green corded cotton completed the furnishings of the room.

Next to Karl's office on the second floor was Käthe's studio, a small room. In the corner she set up a solid work-table, laying bowls, paper, tools, and copper plates on it in small groupings. She scrubbed accumulated dust and dirt from the floor and the walls, and removed the pictures which hung on the dull surfaces. After this, no pictures hung there, for she preferred to work in a plain room, free of visual distractions.

They had been married but a few months when Jeep, still studying in Munich, came to visit Käthe. Jeep did not know if it was still acceptable to call Käthe "Schmidt," as she always had.

> Schmidt insisted that it should be the way it always had been. Our attitude toward life was that of a child's: we still expected adventures. At the very first meeting with Käthe's husband, who now belongs to both of us, we laughed and laughed hysterically. We were taken by such a storm of laughter that we barely needed any reason or impulse to start us up again! Dr. Kollwitz was helpless. Finally he diagnosed it—and us—as fatigue, and told

us that we should go to sleep. So we retreated to the big double bed, and the unstoppable laughter succumbed, after a while, to our dreams.[9]

The Kollwitz marriage, in the beginning, "endured stormy fights, and lacked sentimentality, and the expected behavior of a young married couple. This certainly had to do with the fact that we were far away from Königsberg."[10]

Indeed, her first self-portrait with Karl, *Junges Paar* (*Selbstbildnis*) [Young Couple (Self-portrait)], an etching she made in 1893, projects a candid image of unsolved emotional strife.* The young marrieds do not touch; a corner of the double bed separates them; they face in opposite directions. The self-absorbed young woman, Käthe, sits at the edge of the bed, stunned by the knowledge of some uncomfortable but immutable truth. She sits forward, her forearms resting on her thighs in a masculine pose, her very large hands close to one another, some fingers touching, over the great folds of her black, ankle-length dress. Her feet are planted wide apart; the drape of her dress, from her thighs to the floor, creates the lines of a massive box. There is a fatefulness to her gaze that gives her face a quality of sad introspection; the alert countenance looks inward; the more she stares, the more she realizes.

Though Karl is present in the work, he stands in the background, at the foot of the bed, his back to us. One of his large hands firmly grips the other behind his back, perhaps in a gesture of defiance. Both seem to be rooted eternally to the spot, static figures who cannot move toward or away from each other. The gray bedroom has a single oval frame on the wall: it may be a mirror, or a frame with no picture; if the latter, perhaps it symbolizes their empty life together, or perhaps Käthe's projection of a bleak married future.

In all, she made three compositions of *Young Couple.* In the first, a charcoal drawing, Käthe appears pregnant, but this is not obvious in the second or third version. Both the first and the second composition (an etching with drypoint

---

*The graphic reproduction in these pages is not the first 1893 etching, but the final, 1904 version of "Young Couple."*

62

done in 1893), she executed within the first two years of marriage. The last is an etching with aquatint that she made in 1904, eleven years later, probably as a final, technical exercise, for the technique of the 1893 etching is uneven, although it dramatizes the raw discord of the couple very well, and perhaps even more successfully than the later, "finished" version.

From the start of their marriage, both Karl and Käthe worked. Karl spent most of his time at his clinic and was "soon burdened with a great deal of work."[11] Käthe drew numerous studies of hands; a young nude woman (probably Jeep); and some self-portraits; and reworked a tavern study for her planned graphic series, *Germinal*. The industrious atmosphere of their first home, like that of her childhood, was conducive to creative work. In fact, she saw these years of their "quiet, hardworking life" as "unquestionably good for my further development."[12]

She followed the rigorous discipline she had practiced as a student, beginning work early in the morning, and stopping in mid- or late afternoon. She continued with her drawing and attempted to improve her etching. Requiring quiet for concentration, she demanded absolute silence from her family when she was working, and was therefore sometimes called a tyrant.[13]

But quiet was elusive, for most of Karl's clientele, waiting next door, were babies, children, and mothers of the working class—in Käthe's estimation, the most beautiful subjects to draw. When she did not have quiet, which was so often the case, she went next door and drew poor women as they waited to visit her husband.

Käthe also fulfilled the duties of a housewife, although she never considered this "real" work—a highly individualistic, unpopular attitude for a woman of her day. She regarded the tasks of housework as unfulfilled chores that never ended, producing no finished product or satisfying sense of accomplishment. On the other hand, she felt that her drawings and etchings constituted fruitful, rewarding work of lasting worth.

During Käthe and Karl's first autumn together, Käthe became pregnant. Considering the widespread ignorance of birth control methods (even within the medical profession), it is highly unlikely that this pregnancy was planned. In the only written record of her first pregnancy Käthe is looking forward to having a child, though she sounds defensive. In September 1891, she wrote Jeep, "I feel queasy, but that is how it is supposed to be the first month. But don't tell [the other art students] about it; they would use it as an excuse against getting married."[14]

When she was a few months pregnant, Käthe etched a beautiful self-portrait. In *Selbstbildnis* [Self Portrait] (1892), she stands nearly full-length before us, her right hand by her side, her left hand lying gently across her breasts; she gazes out dreamily, preoccupied with a distant image. Unlike any of her other self-portraits, this one conveys a light, drifting mood.

As she became fuller, she designed an etching, *Begrüssung* [Greeting], to mark the occasion of the birth of her first child. In May 1892, she began to feel labor pains while this plate was still immersed in acid. She left the studio and, hours later, under her own roof, gave birth to a boy. The infant, whom they named Hans, thus arrived almost simultaneously with *Greeting*. She attributed the over-darkness of this print to Hans' birth, for during her labor pains the plate had been submerged too long in the acid. In this overtreated print—a quiet, joyous composition—the mother hands the baby to the father with pride and gratitude, as if it were her gift to him. Of her many family portraits, *Greeting* is the one picture in which she centers attention on the father.

Käthe soon began to use little Hans as a model, sketching at least eighteen studies of her first son. Although Käthe had to care for Hans' constant needs, Karl "did everything possible so that I would have time to work."[15] As soon as they could afford it, a live-in housekeeper was hired to deal with the time-consuming housekeeping and child-rearing duties.

The housekeeper, Lina Mäkler, a woman of about Käthe's age, was of immeasurable help to the artist. She quickly became an integral part of the Kollwitz household, helping as a morning and afternoon babysitter, as an early-morning and dinner cook, and as a general housekeeper for their very tidy apartment. It was common for many middle-class families—

(*text continued on page 68*)

PLATE 5. Käthe Kollwitz.

PLATE 6. *Junges Paar* (Selbstbildnis) [Young Couple (Self-portrait)],
1904, etching.

PLATE 7. Käthe Kollwitz and Karl Kollwitz.

if they did not include unmarried sisters—to have a live-in housekeeper who cared for the household over a long period of time, often the duration of her employers' lifetime, as was the case with Lina. Housekeeping offered room and board and some job security for single working-class women, and many preferred housekeeping—demanding though it was—to dismal, back-breaking factory work.

Despite the preoccupations of her first year of mother-hood, Käthe tried to place some of her work in shows. "My occasional efforts to exhibit failed. But in connection with one of these exhibitions, a show of the rejected applicants was arranged, and I took part in this."[16]

The first public criticism of her work slandered her sex. The leading "establishment" art critic Ludwig Pietsch belittled the entire show by pointing out that one of its artists was a woman, quoting a misogynist couplet from Käthe's favorite poet, Goethe, that "when the road leads to an evil place, woman has a head start in the race."[17]

In direct oppostion to Pietsch was Julius Elias, who wrote:

> In almost every respect the talent of a young woman stands out. A young woman who will be able to bear the insult of this first rejection lightly, for she is assured of a rich artistic future. Frau Kollwitz perceives nature readily and intensely, using clear, well-formed lines. She is attracted to unusual light and deep color tones. [Hers is] a very earnest display of artwork.[18]

For this praise of her work—which was dark in spirit and style, like the work of Edvard Munch, whose pictures had caused a sensation the year before—Elias was branded "an idiot"[19] by Pietsch. The dark, Nordic sensibility of Kollwitz and Munch was new to the Berlin art world. Acclaimed by some, it was downgraded by others.

Unfortunately, the Berlin art world had changed little since Käthe had been there as a student seven years earlier; it was still dominated by unfeeling, academic strictures and insipidly bourgeois tastes. In opposition to this "establish-ment" a group of younger artists, with socialist politics and vaguely expressionistic views of art—the primacy of feeling over form—formed Die Sezession (The Secession). It is probable that Kollwitz was the only female member of The Secession when it was founded. At the group's first exhibit, which was free and open to the public, she contributed two pastel drawings and one etching.

At this time she made two other etchings, *An der Kirchenmauer* [By the Churchyard Wall] and *Betendes Mädchen* [Girl Praying]. Though *Girl Praying* and other works have contributed to her reputation as a "religious artist," she did not so identify herself.

While she had rejected "everything that went by the name of religion,"[20] in the formal sense, when her grandfather died, Käthe found that she could not dissociate herself from the influence of his strong religious spirit. When questioned about this, she wrote:

> Although I thought that Grandfather's religious force did not live on in me, a deep respect remained, a respect for his teachings, his personality and all that the Congregation stood for. I might say that in recent years I have felt both Grandfather and Father within myself, as my origins. Father was nearest to me because he had been my guide to socialism, socialism in the sense of the longed-for brotherhood of men. But behind that concept stood Rupp, whose traffic was not with humanity, but with God. He was the religious man.
>
> To this day I do not know whether the power which has inspired my works is something related to religion, or is indeed religion itself. I am curious to see what you make of it. I know only that it actually is a power. . . .[21]

Religious or not, what is certain is that Kollwitz possessed a spiritual intensity that pervades all the people she drew, moving us to share in their sufferings and their occasional joys—as she herself did: "I have never done any work cold. . . . I have always worked with my blood, so to speak."[22]

On February 28, 1893, she attended a stirring performance, the première of a great play, *Die Weber* [The Weavers] by Gerhart Hauptmann, the poet she had dined with in Berlin ten years before. Despite a Berlin police ban on all public performances of this play, Berlin's most talented theater company, the Berliner Freie Bühne [The Independent Stage Company of Berlin] performed the work. The drama told the story of a group of Silesian peasants turned linen weavers, who, just fifty years earlier, in 1844, had revolted because of their low factory wages and wretched living conditions.

> The performance was given in the morning. I no longer remember who got me a ticket. My husband's work kept him from going, but I was there, burning with anticipation. The impression the play made was tremendous. The best actors of the day participated, with Else Lehmann playing the young weaver's wife. In the evening there was a large gathering to celebrate, and Hauptmann was hailed as the leader of youth.[23]

Käthe strongly identified with the emotions of the weavers, particularly as they chanted to their bosses, "Let Jaeger come out, let Jaeger come out! Let Hoelz come out!" boldly demanding an eye for an eye, a tooth for a tooth.[24] The effect of these mass scenes was so overwhelming that Käthe, too, became filled with the weavers' passionate cry for revenge. "That performance was a milestone in my work. I dropped the series on *Germinal* and set to work on *The Weavers*."[25] She was thus transformed, overnight, into an artist who celebrated revolution. Just as she had used Freiligrath's poems and Zola's *Germinal*, she now used Hauptmann's sourcebook[26] to help her visualize the people, conditions, and events that had helped shape the weavers' revolt. She did not illustrate Hauptmann's version but used it as raw material for her own highly dramatic scenes of the revolt.

"My work on this series was slow and painful";[27] perhaps, for this reason, Käthe termed it "the child of sorrow." For the next five years it absorbed her completely. She organized the revolt into six frames: 1) *Not* [Poverty] ; 2) *Tod* [Death] —a weaver's child dies of hunger; 3) *Beratung* [Conspiracy] —the weavers plan to avenge their child's death; 4) *Weberzug* [Weavers on the March]—to the factory owner's home; 5) *Sturm* [Attack]—on the boss's mansion by the weavers' community;

6) *Ende* [The End]—the revolt, and the lives of some of the men, are over.

Recalling the fire of the weavers' righteousness, Käthe worked long and hard to depict the scenes in the truest manner. She must have relied heavily upon her youthful studies of Königsberg's *Jimkes*, who seemed to her to be "classic" in a way the Berlin workers were not.

> The type of workman to be found [in Berlin] was entirely different from the kind which had interested me. The Berlin worker stood on a much higher economic plane than the Koenigsberg worker, and as far as the visual aspects of his personality went, he was useless as a subject to me.[28]

As she turned back to her Königsberg impressions, a study of a room became helpful. *Königsberger Kneipe* [Königsberg Tavern], done in 1890-91, appears later in *Conspiracy* as the corner of the pub where four weavers sit huddled in talk.

Her work on "the child of sorrow" made Käthe painfully aware of how little etching technique she actually had; her training had been too brief, and insufficient. "At the time I had so little technique that my first attempts were failures."[29] Finally, after many disappointing attempts to etch the series, she decided to lithograph some of the prints.

She brought up a small stone to her studio and began the lithographic process. Having prepared the stone by grinding it down, she drew on it with a greasy lithographic crayon. Next, she covered the slab with gum arabic. This done, she dampened the entire slab, then rolled ink onto the stone so that it would take to the drawn lines and areas, but not adhere to the watered parts. After many pulls, the first three lithographs, *Poverty*, *Death*, and *Conspiracy*, printed well. Revitalized, she finished the last three frames as etchings. It is more acceptable, by professional standards, for a graphic series to consist of one medium; however, because she was not—at least, in her own highly critical opinion—technically competent in etching, and because she was determined to complete it, *Ein Weberaufstand* [The Revolt of the Weavers] is made up of three lithographs and three etchings.

She used four more processes—drypoint, aquatint, tusche wash and soft ground—to perfect the etching. As

*71*

Werner Timm has noted, her training as a painter can be readily seen in *The Revolt of the Weavers*, for by employing a variety of processes, Kollwitz achieved the subtleties of light and line characteristic of painting.[30]

Drypoint entailed engraving directly onto the hard-ground surface of the plate with a steel pencil, which created a burr, or shaving, of copper at the sides of the engraved furrow. This method, which determines how much ink is bled onto the print, comes close to achieving the direct effect of pen and ink; upon printing, the technique produced fine, sharp lines.

For the opposite effect of rounded lines and areas, she used soft ground, which, unlike hard ground, remains malleable and pliant after drying. The copper plate was coated with the special ground of tallow and asphalt, but now, instead of drawing into the wax, she placed a sheet of thin paper on top of the ground and drew directly on this. When printed, part of the wax ground stuck to the paper, creating a grainy effect.

Aquatint was a more primitive procedure. Required were a cardboard box with an air-tight lid, bellows, and a bag of rosin, the distilled resin from the crude oil of turpentine. First, Käthe punctured a small hole in the side of the box. Then she covered the copper plate with heated wax-asphalt. She did not blacken the the plate with candle smoke, but placed the warm plate in the box, waxed side up, and quickly closed the lid. Now she fit the bellows into the hole and slowly pumped air into the resin bag, carefully blowing the resin over the thinly waxed plate, so that some of the resin—microscopic particles with hard edges—penetrated the soft wax to the plate and melted. When the wax was removed from the plate, these melted resin particles remained. Then, the plate was etched by acid in those areas not speckled by the resin, and when the printer's ink flowed onto the plate, a fine, uneven dimensional shading resulted.

Kollwitz' meticulous craft and her aesthetic and political vision of the working-class man and woman are apparent in *The Revolt of the Weavers*. The first lithograph, *Poverty*, pictures a crowded room in which a child is sleeping in a bed in the foreground. The mother, with deeply wrinkled brow, is stooped over the bed, her large, bony hands clutching her

72

head in despair. Father and another child sit huddled by the back window, anxiously watching the sleeping child. The small window lightens the sleeping child's face, but only partially draws out the features of the watching family. The parents' steady gaze at their sick child reflects uneasy despair. An empty loom, ominous sign of unemployment, fills the back of the room.

The next print, *Death*, squares the mother, the father, and the grinning skull of death in a cramped, candle-lit cubicle. Death's fleshy arm is wrapped around the neck of the dumb, staring child; the other arm, a skeleton, barely tugs on the woman's forearm. The mother slumps away from the child, the candle, and Death, in unspeakable grief. Only one ear, the cheek, and the drawn, thin-lipped mouth of the mother are lit by the candle. The father stands opposite her in the right foreground, his large back to us. His figure and head are black, except for his slight, side-angled profile, turned disbelievingly toward his child's wide-eyed face. The entire composition, except for the illuminated face of the dead child, is in black or in darkening shades of gray.

*Conspiracy* pictures four men huddled nose to nose in a corner table of a pub. A weak light hanging above casts long, dark shadows over them and the table. One man on the right draws the most light from the lamp, the most attention from his mates. He leans over the table, both fists clenched; his intent gaze encompasses his friends, but does not see them—he is looking at something, somewhere beyond them. The man next to him, also lighted in profile, rests a tight fist on the table; he watches his friend intensely, ready for his next word. Next to him sits a man we cannot see except for his right arm, draped around the chair of a fourth. The fourth man, back to us, leans halfway over the table to meet his fellows in plans which no other ears will hear. Two empty beer mugs sit abandoned on the table. The men's caps hang beside an eerie hangman's noose above their heads. The floor, table, and walls are wide, heavy wooden planks. The mood is taut with fearful, yet brave, decision-making.

*Weavers on the March* catches eighteen different faces in a wave of revolutionary passion. Some explode with rebellious fire; others fall silent, troubled and afraid, but determined. All are desperate. In the foreground walks a lean woman, staring at the ground, her head and back bent under the weight of a sleeping child on her back. In front of her walks an angry man, holding his fist clenched to his chest in a gesture of fierce determination. Behind him a young woman marches between two men, one young, one old. The young woman stares fixedly ahead. The young man, head high, joins others in shouts and songs. The old man's downturned mouth scowls in bitter righteousness; his hands sit deep and square in his jacket pockets. Behind these three march a line of strong, tall men. One shouts; the others look ahead, at the ground, or at the other marchers. The four different angles of their heads create a dynamic marching pace for the entire picture. Those behind and around them carry weapons—axes, picks, and scythes—wave their fists defiantly, or stare resignedly into space. All wear clogs and plain work jackets and dresses. Strong hatching and detail lines create a powerful impression of angry, determined working people.

In *Attack* women, children, and men in the foreground hand stones to men battering at the ornate wrought-iron gates in the background. From the ground inlay a man and a child pry stones, which they hand to a woman who is bending low in the center foreground; she packs them into her apron with one hand, with the other passing them to a man poised to hurl them over the high stone wall. Another man, full of anger, stretches out an open palm to grab a rock from her. Men and women are shaking and hacking at the heavy bars of the gates. The people's pure, earthy anger contrasts sharply with the iron gates' ornate curves. *Attack* is a monument to revolutionary wrath.

*The End* draws us back into a dark interior. Two men lie dead in the middle of the broad-planked wooden floor. A woman sits by the head of one of the dead, her large hands hugging her knees, her head sunk deep in her breasts. A third dead man is being carried by two comrades through the door to the right. They both stop at the door, aghast at their mates on the floor. A woman stands by the door, her head turned toward the new arrival; her face is stern, her hands loosely but resolutely rounded in fists. Her posture and face, both in full light, reflect deep, contained grief. A window behind her admits some glimmering of light; and one strong beam, directly behind her head, stretches from door to window. In this last frame the light focuses on the woman's pose, rather than on the dead men. As Otto Nagel has noted, *Poverty*, *Death*, *Conspiracy*, and *The End* show excellent use of chiaroscuro[31] (the application of light and shade). One of the discarded sketches Kollwitz made of the woman showed her posed with her hands folded in front of her, a gesture of resignation. The hands held down straight by her sides, however, more clearly indicate simple dignity, strength, and self-containment in grief.

*The Revolt of the Weavers* was noteworthy as a graphic series in which working people initiate, execute, and suffer the fate of their own uprising. It was also a departure from the usual view of working women. Although the women do not plan the attack with the men, they participate in the battle— they grieve, march, fight bravely—and it is they who stand stalwart in loss. Finally, and perhaps most significantly, Kollwitz' "child of sorrow" presented the death of a child as the force that drove a community of workers to revolt.

In 1896, in the midst of her work on *The Revolt of the Weavers*, Käthe bore her second son, Peter. The arrival of another baby added to her burdens but also stimulated her creativity. Each of her involvements energized her in another. In spite of her "wretchedly limited working time," she observed, "I was more productive because I was more sensual; I lived as a human being must live, passionately interested in everything."[32]

That summer, as she completed the series, her father became critically ill. Her parents moved to Rauschen so that he could recuperate in the hearty salt air. Käthe traveled by coach and train to show her first graphic work to her father, dedicated to him, on his seventieth birthday. "He was overjoyed. I can still remember how he ran through the house calling again and again to Mother to see what little Kaethe had done."[33] She must have been especially pleased that her father liked the series, for it showed that she had successfully managed the three lives of artist, wife, and mother. But

in the spring of the following year he died. I was so depressed because I could no longer give him the pleasure of seeing the work publicly exhibited that I dropped the idea of a show. A good friend of mine,

75

Anna Plehn, said, "Let me arrange everything." She entered the series for me, sent it in to the jury, and a few weeks later it was in the show at the Lehrter Station.[34]

In the Great Berlin Exhibit of 1898 it created a sensation among public and critics alike. Käthe confided in Jeep that

the child of sorrow sold on the third day. When I heard this I was so surprised that I stood still with my mouth open. Five hundred marks! [$118.79 in U.S. dollars at the time]. And this for printing only one copy, and not for plates. It is amazing.[35]

The most famous artist of the day, eighty-three-year-old Adolf Menzel, was so impressed with the artistry of *The Revolt of the Weavers* that he proposed, as a member of the jury, to award the prestigious Gold Medal to Kollwitz. But Kaiser Wilhelm II vetoed this nomination, possibly out of his antagonism toward art showing socialist sympathies.

One year later, when the series was shown in Dresden, the Dresden Museum's director of Prints and Drawings, Max Lehrs, proposed to the King of Saxony that Kollwitz be awarded the Gold Medal. The monarch agreed, and in 1899 conferred upon her the highly esteemed award.

In her thirty-second year Käthe was astonished to find that "from then on, at one blow, I was counted among the foremost artists of the country."[36]

## NOTES

1 Kollwitz, *Diary and Letters*, p. 62.
2 *Ibid.*, p. 70.
3 *Ibid.*
4 *Ibid.*, p. 41.
5 *Ibid.*, p. 23.
6 Käthe Kollwitz, *Briefe der Freundschaft*, pp. 20–21.
7 Nagel, *Käthe Kollwitz*, p. 22.
8 *Ibid.*
9 Bonus-Jeep, *Sechzig Jahre*, p. 44.
10 Käthe Kollwitz, *"Ich will wirken in dieser Zeit"* introd. Friedrich Ahlers-Hestermann, ed. Hans Kollwitz (Berlin: Gebrüder Mann Verlag, 1952), pp. 84–85.
11 Kollwitz, *Diary and Letters*, p. 41.

12 *Ibid.*, p. 42.

13 According to Mrs. Arne Kollwitz, wife of Kollwitz' grandson. Interview conducted by Gaby Stöckle, West Berlin, October 15, 1972.

14 Bonus-Jeep, *Sechzig Jahre*, p. 46.

15 Kollwitz, *Diary and Letters*, p. 42.

16 *Ibid.*

17 Translation is by Mina C. and H. Arthur Klein, reprinted with their permission. Mina C. and Arthur Klein, *Käthe Kollwitz: Life in Art* (New York: Holt, Rinehart and Winston, Inc., 1972), p. 29.

18 Heilborn, *Die Zeichner*, p. 33.

19 *Ibid.*, p. 34.

20 Kollwitz, *Diary and Letters*, p. 163.

21 *Ibid.*, pp. 163-164.

22 *Ibid.*, p. 156.

23 *Ibid.*, p. 42.

24 *Ibid.*, pp. 99-100.

25 *Ibid.*, p. 42.

26 Hauptmann had based his play on Alfred Zimmermann, *The Rise and Fall of the Industry of Linen Weaving in Silesia* (Breslau: W. G. Korn, 1885).

27 Kollwitz, *Diary and Letters*, p. 42.

28 *Ibid.*, pp. 28-29.

29 *Ibid.*, p. 42.

30 Nagel, *The Drawings of Käthe Kollwitz*, p. 9.

31 Nagel, *Käthe Kollwitz*, p. 29.

32 Kollwitz, *Diary and Letters*, p. 53.

33 *Ibid.*, p. 42.

34 *Ibid.*, pp. 42-43.

35 Bonus-Jeep, *Sechzig Jahr*, pp. 57-58.

36 Kollwitz, *Diary and Letters*, p. 43.

# 5

## I was gripped by the full force of the proletarian's fate.

*Käthe stood at the rail* of the tiny balcony, looking three stories down to the jumbled, humming intersection of Weissenburgerstrasse and Wörther Platz. In the early morning sun, the cobblestones shone black, brown, and blue; tall tenements and squat, one-room stores looked more cheerful, washed in light. Shopkeepers let down their front awnings; paper vendors called from kiosks; produce hucksters rolled their large wagons onto the street, shouting out prices to passersby. More and more workers—mostly men—streamed out of their flats and headed for work—on foot or by bicycle, or riding on clattering, horse-drawn trams.

Such activity! The hubbub unnerved Käthe a bit, though she could not say why. Returning to the table, she sipped a cup of coffee, thinking over a recent discussion she had had with Karl and Konrad. Some unsettling facts about the economy had been brought up: German capitalism had now, at the turn of the twentieth century, reached a new peak. The steel, shipbuilding, paper, and chemical industries were booming. Capital flow had greatly increased, and many private, joint-stock, and cooperative concerns were springing up, as banks readily financed loans to old and new businesses. For the first time in history, capitalists were producing a great deal of money both for Germany and for themselves.

And a great deal of misery for the people who ran their machines. Berlin, now two million strong, bulged with Slavic and Prussian peasants, as well as those from other parts of Germany, drawn by the relentless influx of heavy industry. Manual laborers and artisans could not survive the onslaught of heavy industry: it was impossible to work and live in dignity in the jobs and homes available to them. Twelve hours a day former peasants stooped over dull, exhausting, dangerous tasks for low wages. At night, they crowded into drafty, poorly-lit tenements, frequently rank from inadequate sanitation. In every industry, children of twelve and older worked full- or half-time alongside their parents; sometimes, if the parents were refused work, children served as the family breadwinners.

In an effort to help stop this exploitation, Konrad and Eduard Bernstein were organizing workers' trade unions in the Social Democratic Party. The recently displaced poor were thoroughly alienated from German society; they had been deliberately—usually, permanently—ghettoized from the upper classes. In an attempt to alleviate the agony of their lives, the SPD offered them cultural, educational, and social activities. At union meetings, workers, the unemployed, and the discontented, listened to the SPD platform, discussed and organized strikes, or visited with friends. Whether or not the SPD was potentially a revolutionary movement after Marx's design, Kaiser Wilhelm II stationed police at each of its meetings; should the sessions offend the Kaiser's antisocialist sensibilities, the police would break up the crowd.

Käthe was deeply concerned with the conditions protested by the SPD. She began work on an etching that would dramatize the tragic waste of workers' lives. *Zertretene* [The Downtrodden], completed in 1900, portrays three victims of Berlin poverty. In this beautifully detailed etching, a mother, a father, and their small child form a desperate picture of an unending cycle of birth, poverty, and death. The mother, her pregnant abdomen protruding slightly, sits dejected, fondly sifting the baby-fine hair of the child held between her knees. One of the father's muscular hands dangles a hangman's noose, childsize. But he cannot execute the act. He turns away, shielding his face with his large, finely sculptured hand.

In *The Downtrodden*, Kollwitz captured the essence of the early 1900s in the lives of three of its impoverished victims, who become timeless faces of the unspoken pains of the poor. However, they are not "types" or "stereotypes," as some critics of her work would have us believe. A careful examination of her work reveals that, although she frequently used the same models (including herself), the inner life of each subject has its own existence: Kollwitz' subjects become universal not because they are "types," but because they express a mood so intensely that all who view it share the feeling. The argument that her subjects are "types" may very well be class-biased. If oppressed people "all look alike" to middle-class and upper-class viewers, then indeed her subjects (in their eyes) may represent "types." But in fact, Kollwitz had a genius for creating particular people, feelings, and scenes.

Her aim was to create beauty; but her idea of beauty differed radically from the aesthetic standards of her day.

> My real motive for choosing my subjects almost exclusively from the life of the workers was that only such subjects gave me in a simple and unqualified way what I felt to be beautiful. For me the Koenigsberg longshoremen had beauty; the Polish *Jimkes* on their grain ships had beauty; the broad freedom of movement in the gestures of the common people had beauty. Middle-class people held no appeal for me at all. Bourgeois life as a whole seemed to me pedantic. The proletariat, on the other hand, had a grandness of manner, a breadth to their lives.[1]

Kollwitz' first motivation to work always sprang from feelings—her own, or those she could clearly grasp in others—and working-class people, "in their native rugged simplicity,"[2] allowed themselves to be seen as they were. Those who concealed themselves—in clothes, cosmetics, class, education, or convention—did not interest her, either personally, or as subjects of her art; they seemed to her not quite "human"—an uncharacteristically harsh judgment for Kollwitz.

> I have never been able to see beauty in the upper-class, educated person; he's superficial; he's not

natural or true; he's not honest, and he's not a human being in every sense of the word.[3]

Above all, working-class women appealed to Kollwitz' aesthetic. Her work shows frank appreciation of their bodies.

> The working-class woman shows me, through her appearance and being, much more than the ladies who are totally limited by conventional behavior. The working-class woman shows me her hands, her feet and her hair. She lets me see the shape and form of her body through her clothes. She presents herself and the expression of her feelings openly, without disguises.[4]

Perhaps there was a degree of self-love in Kollwitz' attraction to working-class women, for she had many of the qualities she admired in them. She favored simplicity in her own appearance, preferring comfortable, tailored dresses, wearing her hair cut short in her younger days, and, during this period, in a bun. Though she came from a so-called "better" class than working women, it was not in her to "put on airs": she was straightforward and honest, and talked plainly.

At this time, shortly after the turn of the century, Käthe began to concentrate on making studies of working women—their faces, hands, and bodies—and gradually, over the years, their images, along with her own, came to be the core of her work.

She drew the women she saw daily, in quick charcoal pen or pencil studies, beautiful and immediate. Some of the women modeled for her, others she drew in her husband's waiting room, and some she sketched in the neighborhood. The sketches include countless female nudes and striking studies of heads. *Frauenkopf* [Head of a Woman], exquisite in its light and dark contrasts, clearly communicates the subject's worried, thoughtful mood. Another subject throws up her hands in a gesture of despair. Ten portraits of a Frau Nitsche reveal the artist's appreciation of this model's beauty, as well as her sensitivity to the woman's troubles. *Frau, auf einer Bank sitzend* [Woman Sitting on a Bench] shows a woman, probably waiting in the clinic, sitting on the edge of her seat, looking at us challengingly. *Sitzende alte Frau beim Kartoffelschälen*

[Old Woman Sitting and Peeling Potatoes] shows the subject leaning tiredly against a doorsill as she works. Two other women—like Käthe, in their mid-thirties—are burdened with worry and children: *Scheltende Frau* [A Scolding Woman] holds her youngest baby tight as she upbraids another child; *Mutter mit zwei Kindern* [Mother with Two Children] sits next to her young boy, with a tot cuddled asleep in her lap, as she looks indifferently into space. Another study is a close-up of the thin, high-cheekboned face of a humble *Heimarbeiter* [Homeworker], who speaks to us not with her lips, but with sad, wistful eyes.

Kollwitz submitted *Homeworker* as a poster to the 1905 German Home Industries Exhibition. But the woman's forlorn expression did not fit the image that industrial Germany wanted to project, so before the Kaiserin would visit the show, orders were given to remove this poster. (The aesthetic taste of the Kaiserin was like that of her husband, who called Kollwitz' work "art of the gutter.")

At this time Kollwitz was obsessed by the theme of woman as revolutionary. In *Aufruhr* [Uprising] (an etching done with aquatint in 1899), desperate, impassioned peasants—all men—march in revolt; hovering overhead, a nude female, the embodiment of revolution and their intangible inspiration, cries out, brandishing a flaming torch. Here Kollwitz herself is the model for the muse of revolution.

Woman as the muse or inspiration for action—rather than as *herself* the actor—is a familiar male concept; and woman as the muse of revolution is a familiar romantic image (Delacroix's *Liberty Leading the People* offers an apt illustration). But it was not this tame concept of the woman revolutionary that Kollwitz was seeking. *Uprising* did not satisfy her.

At this point Kollwitz began reading Charles Dickens' *A Tale of Two Cities* and other accounts of the French Revolution, in which peasants and bourgeoisie had revolted against the decadent monarchy of King Louis XVI. Peasant and Parisian women alike participated in the revolution, despite male opposition. In 1791, a huge group of Parisian women marched eleven miles to the palace of King Louis XVI in Versailles; there they surrounded the building and forced him and his family to return to Paris as hostages. A few years later, the all-female battalions were "officially" banned; in spite of this, they continued to form. In *A Tale of Two Cities*, Dickens wrote of one such band of women:

> . . . there was no other music than their *own* singing. They danced to the popular revolution song, keeping a ferocious time that was like a gnashing of teeth in unison.[5]

The most popular song of the French Revolution was "La Carmagnole"—"Dansons La Carmagnole, Vive le son du canon!" ("O, let us dance the Carmagnole, Long live the sound of the cannon!")—and it was with this theme, sung and danced by peasant women, that Kollwitz depicted the French Revolution. In *Die Carmagnole* peasant women rhythmically dance, sing, and keen around the center guillotine at a feverish pitch. These women revolutionaries did not fight in conventional roles, as adjuncts of men, protecting and assisting them, but in their *own* battalions, with a militancy equal to that of the men. They took the ideals of the revolution seriously, considering the revolution "the liberty and responsibility of every human being, limited only by the rights of all, without privilege of race or sex."[6]

In this etching and aquatint, finished in 1901, cramped Parisian tenements surround ragged women of all ages, whose bare feet beat the street's big cobblestones. A lone drummer boy stands in the foreground, chanting and drumming the cadence of "La Carmagnole." In this work, more than in any other, Kollwitz demonstrates her lively instinct for the bodily movements and facial expressions created in the rhythm of dance. In fact, she herself loved to dance, "loved liveliness and grace of movement."[7]

Shortly after finishing *Die Carmagnole*—which quickly became popular—Kollwitz read in Zimmermann's *The Great German Peasants' War*, about the peasant woman, Black Anna, who incited the peasants to rebel.[8] Still actively searching for the image of the woman revolutionary, Kollwitz continued to hope "to represent it, to get it out of me."[9] Black Anna supplied her, at last, with the historical prop for this vision. Kollwitz' strong personal identification with Black Anna becomes evident in the four preliminary drawings in which she shaped the subject's body in her own likeness.

Giving the signal for the peasants to revolt, in *Losbruch* [Outbreak], Black Anna throws her strong arms high above her head, as her entire body strains in a thrust of invincible power. Behind Black Anna are the tattered, hapless peasants who spring at her call, instantly turning their rage into an unflinching determination to fight. They race past, bent double, ferocious revenge incarnate in them, carrying scythes, picks, and medieval swords poised at the same jackknife angles as their charging bodies.

Other artists had shown women fighting to defend themselves, their husbands, their homes or children, but no one had ever before depicted a lone woman inciting revolution. With the unforgettable image of Black Anna, Kollwitz once more broke with tradition.

In 1525 Black Anna and other peasants suffered the lot of downtrodden serfs. The landed aristocracy was depriving the peasants free use of meadows and woodland, thereby denying them a long-established right. The serfs had no acreage of their own to till, no money to pay the excessive taxes levied by the nobility, and no civil rights to protect them from the wanton whims of the overlords who "owned" them. Spurred by the example of Luther (who had recently broken with Papal Rome), serfs throughout southern Germany revolted against their lords and the repressive Roman Catholic Church, a large landholder.

Kollwitz achieved the finished beauty of this powerful etching through many takes of aquatint, pen-and-ink wash, and several textures of soft ground. When she was finally satisfied, she submitted *Outbreak* to the Association for Historical Art, and, on the basis of this frame, they commissioned her to complete a series on Germany's Peasant War.

For *Bauernkrieg* [The Peasant War], Kollwitz lithographed and drew many studies, using pencil, charcoal, white crayon, and pastel on chamois paper, and on paper colored yellow, brown, dark gray, and white. Very gradually, in six additional etchings, she delineated the events of The Peasant War. In the first plate, *Die Pflüger* [The Ploughmen], a serf plows a field, harnessed like a beast of burden to a crude, heavy hoe. Then she composed the fourth frame, *Bewaffnung in einem Gewölbe* [Distribution of Weapons in a Vault], in which serfs seize upon weapons as they crowd the spiral stairway of their lord's dungeon armory. Kollwitz made three sketches for the sixth frame, *Schlachtfeld* [Battlefield], in which a mother searches through the black-gray night for her son. Exploring the psychological motivation of the revolt, Kollwitz made, in 1904–1905, ten studies of a working woman as an elderly serf, and these studies she called *Inspiration*. One shows an old woman who tries to stand but is prevented by the weight of a heavy figure leaning on her back, whispering in her ear. Kollwitz rejected this view of inspiration for the revolt in favor of a more human, less mystical and symbolic interpretation—a peasant woman sharpening a scythe with a whetstone, one eye knotted closed while the other, barely opened to a slit, is a blot of blind fury. The peasant woman in *Beim Dengeln* [Whetting the Scythe] seethes with the memory—and presence —of pent-up humiliation.

Kollwitz' responsibilities as a mother and wife, and her own moods, forced her to abandon work on *The Peasant War* for months at a time. Also, as a result of the reputation she was acquiring as a fine etcher and lithographer, she had been asked to teach graphic arts and life (nude) drawing.

At first Kollwitz declined the offer made by the Berlin School of Art for Women—which she had attended fifteen years earlier—for she felt incompetent to teach etching professionally. Also, she was shy among strangers and accustomed to working in the unbroken solitude of a small, single room. Teaching, in contrast, required a direct social presence as she worked. However, the director, Fräulein Hönerbach, assured Kollwitz that, if necessary, she would help her out.

> That came about very soon. I had to show the class how to make an etching ground. The process was a book with seven seals to me and I perspired with embarrassment as I started to trot out my meager knowledge before the eager girls standing in a group around me. Suddenly I heard Fraeulein Hoenerbach's voice; she had joined the group of students. "Yes, Frau Kollwitz," she said, "that is one way to do it. But I'd like to tell you how Koepping taught me to do it." Then she took the plate and other materials out of my hands and saved the situation for me.[10]

But with the cares of her household and her two children, and the pressures to continue with her own work, she soon decided to drop teaching.

During the winter months she had found that Hans and Peter were sick more often; Peter, especially, was susceptible to lung infections. Now, however, Hans had fallen ill. Karl diagnosed Hans' illness as diphtheria and injected him with an unperfected but popular serum that had healed many in the last epidemic of diphtherial throat infection. After the injection Hans grew stronger, and Karl considered him nearly well. Suddenly, a week later, the boy's condition worsened alarmingly. The anxious parents tended him all through the night.

> Finally, in the middle of the early morning, at three A.M., my husband said, "I think we've won him back." . . . During this night an unforgettable cold chill caught and held me: it was the terrible realization that any second this young child's life may be cut off, and the child gone forever. . . . It was the worst fear I have ever known.[11]

Months later, the long moments of this night would return to her; she would relive the awful knowledge of mortal—and parental—helplessness. At last she confronted Hans' touch with death in the creation of *Frau mit totem Kind* [Woman with Dead Child]. Though Hans had been its inspiration, she used Peter as a model for this piece.

> When he was seven years old and I was doing the etching *Mother with Dead Child*, I drew myself in the mirror while holding him in my arm. The pose was quite a strain, and I let out a groan. Then he said consolingly in his high little voice: "Don't worry, Mother, it will be beautiful, too."[12]

The finished etching was so painfully real that some viewers (her best friend, Jeep, included) could not face it. It pictures a small, limp child, head fallen back, almost totally engulfed in the grasp of the nude mother's body and limbs. The mother's face and mouth disappear into the child's chest as if to warm him, to breathe her life into his. No clothes or background, past or friends comfort her; her child's death has stripped the mother to the raw edge of existence.

Hans' brush with death was the sole personal trauma in this decade of Käthe's life. She wrote, "My life between thirty and forty was very happy in every respect. We had sufficient to live on; the children were growing up and healthy; we went traveling."[13]

As a mother, Käthe was in some respects not unlike the woman who had raised her. One of the characteristics she shared with Katharina was a disinclination to show her children love and affection in a physical way. Hans later wrote:

> Both of us boys, myself and my brother Peter, who was four years younger than I, loved our home and above all loved our mother. But we loved her with that naturalness with which young animals as well as human beings love their mothers. While the feeling itself remains perfectly natural, the children never doubt that their mother is there for them and there is no talk of love at all. Love was simply there, felt but not shown; and our mother was not given to demonstrativeness.[14]

Käthe admitted that she never had a "way" with her sons when they were toddlers, but by the time they had reached the ages of six and nine she had begun to enjoy their company more, especially because she could now contribute to their intellectual development. In temperament Hans was like Käthe—quiet and serious, and inclined to melancholy. Peter, on the other hand, was an extrovert with a good sense of humor, many friends, and diverse interests. Their mother was a great companion "in our fantastic games, especially when these games were linked up with her own childhood."[15] She designed kites for them, had an acrobatic bar installed in their hallway, taught them gardening (which Peter, especially, loved), acted in their amateur theatricals, and took them on long country walks on weekends.

> It was also wonderful to go traveling with Mother, or to take walks with her—to be out in the open with her at all. At such times she was usually quiet; when we were out to see things, she wanted to see, not talk. But often she was so happy that, as she did once on a short trip to Rheinsberg, she would walk

hand in hand with me, singing folksongs. She loved
nature, especially the picturesque aspects of nature,
and she drank in whatever she saw. But on none of
these trips which I made with her did I ever see her
drawing. Nature did not arouse her creative drive.
That was why she found so much relaxation in it.[16]

She enjoyed these weekend jaunts with family and
friends, but the most vividly recollected trips she took on her
own.

Käthe's first opportunity to travel alone was in 1904 at
the invitation of two friends, Lily and Dr. Heinrich Braun,
who were collaborating on a new socialist art journal called
*Die Neue Gesellschaft* [The New Society]. Käthe readily
accepted their invitation to visit them in Paris, for she and Karl
had visited the city briefly a few years before, and she had
been wanting to return for a longer stay.

Paris enchanted me. In the mornings I went to the
old Julien School for the sculpture class, in order to
familiarize myself with the fundamentals of sculpture. Afternoons and evenings I visited the wonderful museums of the city, the cellars around the markets or the dance-halls on Montmartre or the Bal
Bullier. One of my friends and fellow artists, Ida
Gerhardi, went there night after night to make
sketches. The cocottes knew her, and when they
were dancing they handed her their things to
watch.[17]

Käthe also sketched some of these scenes; she did drawings of
a cellar restaurant called Caveau des Innocents—Cave of
the Innocents, which she titled these sketches—and twelve
drawings of Parisians sitting on benches and in cafés.

Two of her Munich classmates, Sophie Wolff and Maria
Slavona, had also settled in the art capital of the Western
world. Dining with Sophie at one of the popular artist cafés on
the Boulevard Montparnasse, Käthe met artists from around
the world. Maria had married the knowledgeable art dealer,
Otto Ackermann, and through him Käthe met the owners of
the private galleries. Another classmate from Munich, Frau
Gretor, also lived in Paris, but in poverty, not glamour, with

her eleven-year-old son, Georg. Käthe was touched by her friend's desperate situation and decided, quite gratuitously and matter-of-factly, to provide Georg with another, more substantial home: her own in Berlin. Georg's mother evidently trusted Käthe as a sister, for she accepted her offer, and Georg soon afterward became a member of the Kollwitz household.

While in Paris Käthe visited the sculpture studio of Auguste Rodin in Meudon. The master's vibrant, sensual, and classically styled sculptures made a deep impression on her:

> I shall never forget that visit. Rodin himself was taken up with other visitors. But he told us to go ahead and look at everything we could find in his atelier. In the center of a group of his big sculptures the tremendous Balzac was enthroned. He had small plaster sketches in glass cases. It was possible to see the full scope of his work, as well as to feel the personality of the old master.[18]

Too soon it was time to leave Paris for Berlin. Käthe had planned to visit Brussels to see Constantin Meunier, the only other well-known socialist artist in graphics, but, "Unhappily, I never carried out this intention. Paris held me fast until the very last evening."[19] When Max Lehrs had shown Meunier some of her work, the Belgian had responded, "I have never seen the hand of a woman create such work!"[20] If Lehrs had not repeated this to Käthe, she had probably read it in a short article he had written on her work in *Die Frau* [Woman], a new magazine launched by bourgeois German women and directed largely to their interests and concerns.

Unfortunately, Meunier's comment reflected the status of women artists, even among socialist men, who were, relatively speaking, more enlightened on "the woman question" than most men of the early 1900s. A decade earlier, in 1890, the SPD had passed a resolution demanding full equality of the sexes; a year later, however, the SPD apparently did not realize that this meant that women should share in the work of the party.[21] Two years later, women were permitted to send delegates to the Annual Congress of the party, and there, under the leadership of Clara Zetkin, the Women's Organization was formed to protect the interests and rights of working-class women.

The Women's Organization was separate from the SPD because socialist women, in common with Zetkin and Bebel, recognized that working-class women were dependent upon working-class men, who were, in turn, dependent upon the capitalists. The women, therefore, could not look to the male members of the SPD for strong efforts on behalf of sexual equality. If the males failed to recognize this chain of dependence, it was because, as Bebel noted, "the question touches his own dear self more or less nearly."[22]

The Women's Organization, its members oppressed by class as well as sex, grew to be the most class-conscious and militant wing of the SPD. It was very popular. At once feminist and socialist, the organization usually met separately from the larger SPD, the majority of whose members were bureaucratic reformists. Socialist women held the feminist view that woman's lowly status is a result of sexism; but as members of the working class, and as socialists, they also believed (with Marx) that by "removing the economic dependence of woman upon man under private property, a new, truly human relationship would be possible under communism."[23] Women of this organization recognized the class and ideological differences between themselves and the bourgeois feminists in Germany, in other European countries, and in America, just as they acknowledged their differences with the SPD. Marxist ideology and practice dominated the Woman's Organization, which now sought to change women's maximum working hours from eleven to ten, and demanded that women not be employed in trades injurious to their health. Their popular biweekly, *Die Gleichheit* [Equality], exposed job, legal, and social service exploitation of working-class women.

Though an ardent socialist, Kollwitz was not a "joiner" of organizations. Probably one of the most political artists of the twentieth century, she was not a political person in the orthodox sense. Politics, as is well known, often entails compromise. One of the great strengths of Kollwitz' character and artistic stance was her refusal to compromise. Indeed, the political content in her work is uncompromising, unequivocal. But her specific "politics" were not easily classified. It is not even known whether she was a member of the SPD Women's Organization—though we do know that she supported women's struggles for equality. Hers was an artist's sensibility, rooted in a deep and complex sense of moral responsibility. An artist first, she was better able to express her unique feminism and socialism daily, in her lone work, rather than as a member of an organization.

In 1907, Max Klinger, her mentor from student days, awarded Kollwitz the Villa Romana prize. With his earnings, Klinger had bought a villa in Florence, to which he invited outstandingly gifted artsits. The artists (and their spouses and children) might live at the villa, cost free, for seven months to a year, absorbing the rich influences of Medieval and Renaissance works of Florentine art.

Käthe would have preferred to visit Paris again, but she accepted Klinger's award gratefully, and brought with her Peter—still weak from a recent bout with tuberculosis. "Aunt Lina," as the boys now affectionately called the housekeeper, cared for Hans and Georg.

Despite the abundance of frescoes, sculpture, architecture, and painting in Florence, Kollwitz found no art of her own. She confessed to a feeling of unending emptiness; with the exception of Michelangelo's work, nothing she saw urged her to draw. During her stay in Florence, Kollwitz produced no work. To Lise she wrote:

> Sometimes I get homesick for my family, but also for all of you. . . . Lately I had the same dream I once had in Paris, that out of homesickness I went home sooner than I was supposed to and that after the joy of welcoming was over I clapped my hand to my head and thought I was mad to have come home earlier than I needed to. So of course I want to stay here until the time is up; but I shall leave here with a lighter heart than I left Paris. Because when it comes down to it, everything here is really alien to me. . . .
>
> The enormous galleries are confusing, and they put you off because of the masses of inferior stuff in the pompous Italian vein. And so I have been trying the churches, with better luck. There are magnificent frescoes in the churches. . . . And finally I again ventured into the Pitti and Uffizi Galleries. There

are beautiful works here and there in them, but only here and there, it seems to me. . . .

As far as the architecture goes, my experience is almost like little Peter's, who impertinently declared that the Palazzo Vecchio is "awful". . . . With Santa Maria Novella, on the other hand, age has entirely erased all the restiveness. The façade of Santa Maria Novella, and the plaza before it, are among the finest things here. . . .

Recently I saw three men standing on a bridge in front of a house, thrumming a guitar and singing to a window above. Suddenly a lovelorn woman's voice began singing a solo; it was one of the men. Whether or not he was a eunuch, I don't know; he did not look it to me. As I stood for a while enjoying it, someone else began singing on a neighboring bridge, and then more and more voices joined in, from right and left, until finally I strolled on home. And then fat Annina [the housekeeper], who is still up, says under her breath with a pitying shake of her head, as she always does: *"Sempre sola, la signora"* [always alone, this woman]. Yes, now I am really *sempre sola.* For a while I liked it, but it is getting to be too much for me.[24]

By another of those delightful coincidences of their friendship, Käthe found herself with Jeep again during this Italian sojourn. Jeep had married a religious writer, Arthur Bonus. (She retained her own last name, a custom among some European women.) Jeep had turned from painting to writing, for which she had a greater gift, often collaborating with her husband. To avoid the exorbitant rents in Germany, the couple had moved to a location near Florence where Jeep had spent her childhood.

Jeep, Peter, and Käthe spent many hot, lazy afternoons together. Unaccustomed to the luxury of Klinger's villa, Käthe felt more comfortable out-of-doors. The two women took long walks, visited Florence, and took Peter for wagon rides through the countryside. Eventually Peter's lungs became stronger; and he returned to Berlin.

*(text continued on page 100)*

PLATE 8. *Die Carmagnole* [The Carmagnole], 1901, etching, sandpaper aquatint.

PLATE 9. *Losbruch* [Outbreak] , 1903, etching.

95

PLATE 10. *Vergewaltigt* [Raped] , 1907, etching and soft ground.

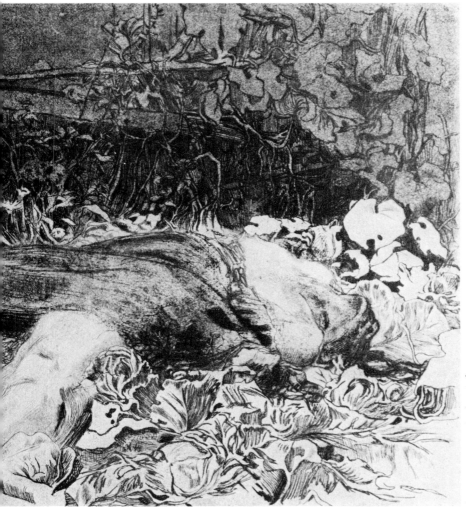

97

PLATE 11. *Beim Dengeln* [Whetting the Scythe] , 1905, etching and soft ground.

PLATE 12. *Nachtasyl* [Shelter for the Night] , 1909, drawing, charcoal.

One stifling, hot afternoon, Käthe and Jeep were perspiring so profusely that Jeep decided to change into a cooler dress. As she did so, she turned her back to Käthe, who was reading in a chair. This nice modesty on the part of Jeep, who in the past had often posed for Käthe, was lost on the artist.

> After a while, when I turned around, I found Schmidt not reading the book, but quietly occupied with watching me. When she found herself caught like this she did not apologize, which I thought she should. But Schmidt was simply not ashamed. Then, when my perplexity turned into laughter, she heartily laughed along with me.[25]

Käthe also spent a great deal of time with an English-woman named Constanza Harding. "Stan," as she preferred to call herself, was slender, athletic, artistically talented, and fearlessly independent; she wore her hair unfashionably short, and spoke fluent German and Italian. At twenty she had run away from her wealthy father, a professional teataster. With little money, but a stubborn will, she had supported herself by tutoring English and copying Florentine art. Stan readily criticized social customs and institutions; she was especially critical of the Church of England, on the grounds that it fostered hypocrisy in its members' personal lives as well as in England's institutions.

Käthe had met Stan through a Dr. Krayl, a German physician of about Käthe's age, who, in the process of being tutored in English by Stan, had fallen in love with her. Stan felt unwilling "to gain a new master so soon after losing the old one," her father.[26] But Dr. Krayl, fearful of jeopardizing his professional reputation by associating intimately with an attractive young woman, at last prevailed upon her to marry him.

At the time Käthe met her, Stan was in a state of misgiving and distress. She had wanted to continue her independent life; but social custom, economic necessity, and the devoted love of a stable man had persuaded her to marry. From the first, Käthe liked Stan's independence; she listened sympathetically to her troubles.

They discovered a mutual love for hiking. After her marriage, Stan had continued to take long walks in the country at all hours, equipped, as always, with a revolver—which her father had taught her to use. Stan suggested that she and Käthe hike through the tiny villages along the coastal route to Rome (approximately one hundred fifty miles). Käthe quickly agreed.

They set out in May, departing in the early evening, for the Italian sun was already intense during the day. Each was wearing sturdy walking shoes and a plain, long dress, and carrying a small bag containing fruit, matches, candles, and maps. Stan was armed with her father's revolver.

Few persons passed their way; the countryside was the loneliest Käthe had ever seen. They hiked past gently rolling hills covered with short wheat grass and scrub brush, fruit trees and grape arbors. Sometimes they passed a shepherd with his flock and his howling sheepdogs; at other times they saw horsemen—lean and tan, wearing wide-brimmed hats and leather jackets, their long guns slung crosswise over the saddle of their emaciated, long-tailed mounts.[27]

Stan's years of hiking had taught her the rule of resting frequently: now and then they paused by the side of the sandy, pebbly road. In the chill of midnight and early morning, they sat back to back for warmth.

They walked into towns that had seldom seen strangers. In one village "the children gathered around . . . numb with terror, until a small girl called out with great relief: 'But they are women.' "[28] Many villagers believed that they were pilgrims on their way to pray for their sins at St. Peter's in Rome. The belief began to seem too difficult to dispel, so Käthe and Stan simply accepted the role.

One morning as the sun was rising, the two entered the tiny sea town of Populonia. They were entirely alone on the village's only street, little more than a lane. The lane led to the Bay of Populonia, framed by a quarter-moon cove. Here, the two seated themselves by the side of an old watchtower, leaning back to watch the changing colors of the sea as the dawn became morning.

Near the watchtower wall lived an eighty-year-old woman, wrinkled with age and the sun. She was taken by surprise at the sight of two women, strangers, sitting quietly near her door, mesmerized by the sun on the sea. Then, mistaking them for pilgrims, she invited them to breakfast. From this village Käthe sent two happy postcards to Jeep.

> I look like leather. I have lost at least ten pounds, and I don't know who has lost more, Stan or I. But it's great, in spite of all the hardships. Two nights ago we hiked straight through the night, and every-thing was there—full moon, lightning bugs, and sing-ing locusts. We walked for hours along the sea as the moon set and the sun rose. . . . In general, though, you can't trust the people around here as much as the people [near Florence], and I see their terrible fright when the revolver is pointed at them. I like Stan more and more; I find her great presence of mind along with her joyfulness very nice.[29]

The two women continued along the shore, over grassy paths and sandy roads; they surveyed the blue-green sea from high, jutting cliffs. It was from the height of some huge boulders they had scaled that they had their first glimpse of the town of Pitigliano.

> One evening we saw the town of Pitigliano lying before us. Like all Umbrian towns, it was so built that from a distance it looked like a long chain of castles. It was situated on a narrow slope, and a single bridge led across to it. We walked across this bridge into the enchanted town, which had only length and no breadth; there were only stubs of narrow lanes to either side of the main road. . . .
>
> On the slope of the town we discovered caves where the people kept their donkeys and other stock. They were Etruscan caves.[30]

The next day Käthe and Stan witnessed the celebration of a high Catholic holiday in Pitigliano. Then, at the suggestion of one of the townspeople, they walked to the site of some ancient ruins. There, amid stone remains of Etruscan gods and goddesses, Käthe and Stan "literally clambered over the limbs of the gods,"[31] picking up stones as souvenirs.

As they continued their trip, they grew anxious to reach Rome, now only a few nights' walk away. They decided to push on nonstop, except for a few long rests and meals. To their own surprise, Käthe and Stan were able to hike through the next two days and nights.

On one of the final days they "took the wrong road and were out of sorts at having to walk all the way back."

> Then a man came along in a little donkey cart that was going back the way we had come. He said we poor pilgrims ought to take a ride, and so we clambered up on the sacks and sat there, eating our cherries and spitting out the pits to right and left of the cart. And the sweet little donkey, whose name was Nina and who had a very big, thick head, trotted along, pulling us.[32]

On June 13, 1907, they entered Rome.[33] Thirty-nine-year-old Käthe arrived exhausted but fulfilled by one of her life's great adventures.

After a few days of rest, Käthe met Hans, excited and proud of his independence in traveling alone by train from Berlin. She showed him as much as possible of Rome and its art treasures in the brief time before the two of them departed to meet Peter and Karl for their family vacation.

That spring, Käthe and Jeep had discovered a picturesque but primitive stone house, situated by the Ligurian Sea, where both families could spend their vacations. Thick, trestled grapevines rising on either side of the stone entrance steps surrounded the building and formed a natural canopy over the outdoor dining room. The house, used by grape harvesters and landscape painters, had none of the customary living facilities. The families built their own latrine, pumped water from a well, cooked on a wood fire, and ate at a stone table with wooden benches.

> After a while Stan and her husband followed us out there and we spent a glorious vacation together. . . . We spent whole afternoons on the water and in the cool grottoes. Once we rowed over to Carrara at dawn, climbed up to the marble quarries and rowed back at night. The night was so quiet that the stars were reflected in the sea and the drops of water fell like glittering stars from the oars.[34]

Finally, reluctantly, the Kollwitzes left this summer haven and returned to Berlin.

At home Käthe reviewed her work on *The Peasant War* and completed the series by drawing three more frames— *Vergewaltigt* [Raped], *Schlachtfeld* [Battlefield], and *Die Gefangenen* [The Prisoners].

*Raped*, the second print of the series, is one of the earliest pictures in Western art to depict a female victim of sexual violence sympathetically and from a woman's point of view. It seems highly likely that the impulse for *Raped* grew directly out of Käthe's hike with Stan, for as women traveling without men they were exposed to the fears and dangers of molestation. In *Raped* a woman lies prostrate, stricken by violence, shock, and humiliation. The foreshortening of her body—with feet in the foreground—is so pronounced that her head and upper torso can scarcely be distinguished. The work presents a protest to the spiritual and physical degradation this act represents for woman. The body, nearly overrun by grass, vines, flowers, and leaves, seems to sink into the ground, decaying before our eyes.

The flowers in *Raped* were the only flowers Kollwitz ever drew. But instead of using them to adorn or decorate, as most of her Impressionist and Postimpressionist colleagues were wont to do, she twined large and small blossoms (the flowers of a cabbage plant from her garden in Berlin) together with brambly vines, around the half-naked body of the violated woman, a victim of mercenaries who roamed their "lord's" countryside. Kollwitz' use of flowers was unorthodox, much as was her use of dance postures: instead of showing men and women on a dance floor (in the customary bourgeois rite of social dancing), she had expressed her interest in dance in *Die Carmagnole* by depicting peasant women dancing around a guillotine in a passionate celebration of revolution. The flowers in *Raped* deepen the shock of the scene.

In *Battlefield*, the sixth plate, a mother, stooped, looks from body to body in the very black of night, searching for her dead son. The last frame, *The Prisoners*, shows rope-bound peasants, mostly men, standing defiant and dignified, in anguish but not in despair, their bare feet planted firmly apart. Unlike the peasants of the last frame in *The Revolt of the Weavers*, these serfs are undefeated, though captive.

Like *The Revolt of the Weavers*, *The Peasant War* depicts revolution and dramatizes the subject from a woman's perspective. Two of the three plates showing the motivation for the Peasant War portray women: one is the "passive" woman, a victim of rape; the other is the "active" peasant woman expressing outrage, her leathery, thick-featured face gnarled with indignation. Black Anna catalyzes the serfs' passions through organized revolt, taking violent action against further humiliation as a serf and as a woman. The last and fifth protagonist is the mother who stoically searches for her son among the dead on a starless night.

None of these women resembled the prevailing standards of feminine beauty. Kollwitz' women work hard in order to survive: their peasant bodies are strong, capable of labor and endurance; they are physical, rather than sexual beings. In this artistic viewpoint—that women have a physical body as opposed to a sexual one—Kollwitz was one of the first to reject the common, timeworn image of women as physically passive, their bodies of interest only as sex objects or as objects of beauty.

But it was not only the physical image that made the women different in *The Peasant War*: Kollwitz gave them positive inner traits. The women have intelligence, courage, dignity, and compassion. One, an older woman, shows fury and, at the same time, deep empathy with the rape of a sister peasant; the revolutionary, Black Anna, has dignity as woman and human in her courageous leadership of revolt; and the mother, while sorrowful, is stalwart in the loss of her son. With these dramatic portraits, Kollwitz projected an unfamiliar, affirmative view of women, especially working-class women, as persons of character and mental ability, fully responsive to the full range of human feeling.

To produce the seven scenes of *The Peasant War*, Kollwitz combined aquatint and soft ground with the regular etching process. Except during her seven-month stay in Florence, she worked faithfully on this final etching series, from 1902 to 1908. *The Peasant War* is larger in size than *The Revolt of the Weavers*, and five of the seven frames lack the superficial stagings of interior props. By this time, Kollwitz was using space like a sculptor: the peasants in this series have more physical depth, and are more their "own persons," standing in open, free space (especially in *Outbreak*). The lasting appeal of the final frame, *Prisoners*, is evidenced in its use, sixty-four years later, by the revolutionary movement in Ireland, which in 1972 added its own touch to the poster: "No More Internment" is printed over the heads of the captured, written in a script resembling Kollwitz'.

When *The Peasant War* was issued in 1908, it confirmed Kollwitz' stature as one of the great graphic artists of Germany. Public and critics alike responded to the monumental composition of the series and its message.

During these years of work on *The Peasant War* Käthe had also been hired as a free-lance artist for the *Simplizissimus*, a progressive Munich monthly with a large circulation. In 1909, the magazine began to publish a series of her drawings collectively entitled *Bilder vom Elend* [Portraits of Misery]. She enjoyed working on these drawings very much. One of the reasons was technical: she was beginning to have an understanding of her artistic powers, and consequently to have more control over them.

> A happy day yesterday. Finished drawing the fifth and last plate for *Simplizissimus*—the Home Industries. Toward evening a pleasant walk as far as the viaduct. I am so glad that I can work well and *easily* now. . . . As a result of so much working on studies I have at last reached the point where I have a certain background of technique which enables me to express what I want without a model.[35]

It was during these years of work for *Simplizissimus* that a *human* concern for the proletariat permanently replaced Kollwitz' aesthetic, academic, and—probably—romanticized interest in the working class. Their troubles were now painfully real to her—she saw them working, living, and struggling every day. When Karl's waiting room was too crowded, as it often was—he was now the second busiest *Kassenarzt* in Berlin—neighborhood women, desperate for help, would walk across the hall to see Käthe.

These visits often sapped her strength. People would bring their griefs and problems to her and usually left feeling relieved. But then *she* would have one more burden to bear. That was the usual way she helped people—although she also helped in a material way, when she was asked to or when she saw that help was needed.[36]

Her poor neighbors found that Käthe, unlike many from the middle class, understood the realities of their lives, and they respected her for this. As a result of these visits, Kollwitz' commitment to the working class became personal.

Much later on, when I became acquainted with the difficulties and tragedies underlying proletarian life, when I met the women who came to my husband for help and so, incidentally, came to me, I was gripped by the full force of the proletarian's fate. Unsolved problems such as prostitution and unemployment grieved and tormented me, and contributed to my feeling that I must keep on with my studies of the lower classes. And portraying them again and again opened a safety-valve for me; it made life bearable.[37]

All the *Simplizissimus* drawings, done with charcoal, tell very directly how working-class women live. Though some critics consider drawing inferior as an art form, it is clear—as Werner Timm has pointed out—that Kollwitz' drawings for the *Simplizissimus* series rank as fully accomplished works of art.[38]

In *Portraits of Misery* working-class women fall faint from hunger—or from beatings by husbands on drinking binges. In the sterile atmosphere of a hospital, the women mourn an infant's death. A pregnant woman knocks on a doctor's door, her head bowed low in shame at her need. At another door an elderly woman begs.

A later drawing for the *Simplizissimus*, *Nachtasyl* [Shelter for the Night], is one of the most strident pictures Kollwitz ever produced. It shows a harried prostitute, flanked on one side by an indifferent working man, on the other by an old woman. The prostitute hugs a client to her. Laughing hysterically, she grabs deep into his pocket for money. His back is to us; neither he nor the others can see her face writhing in a wild, victorious cry. Kollwitz clearly sympathizes with the prostitute, without judging her or the working-class man who is her client. Rather, the drawing is a condemnation of the society that produced the prostitute.

Kollwitz derived great satisfaction from working on the *Simplizissimus.* One hundred marks (then about twenty-four dollars) per drawing was excellent income for free-lance work, and an important supplement to the modest Kollwitz budget; also, Käthe was given free rein as to subject matter and style, along with the challenge of portraying a subject for a large audience. Above all, she liked drawing for the *Simplizissimus* because it gave her frequent opportunities to express to great numbers of people "what always moves me again and again, and what has not been said enough: the many quiet and loud tragedies of city life."[39]

## NOTES

1 Kollwitz, *Diary and Letters*, p. 43.

2 *Ibid.*, p. 4.

3 Agnes Smedley, "Germany's Artist of the Masses," *Industrial Pioneers* (September 1925), p. 9.

4 Heilborn, *Die Zeichner*, p. 28.

5 Charles Dickens, *A Tale of Two Cities* (New York: Airmont Publishing Co., Inc., 1963), p. 238.

6 Sheila Rowbotham, *Women, Resistance and Revolution: A History of Women and Revolution in the Modern World* (New York: Pantheon Books, 1972), p. 105.

7 Kollwitz, *Diary and Letters*, p. 3.

8 *Ibid.*, p. 162.

9 *Ibid.*

10 *Ibid.*, p. 44.

11 Bonus-Jeep, *Sechzig Jahre*, p. 100.

12 Kollwitz, *Diary and Letters*, p. 164.

13 *Ibid.*, p. 44.

14 *Ibid.*, p. 2.

15 *Ibid.*, p. 3.

16 *Ibid.*, p. 6.

17 *Ibid.*, p. 44.

18 *Ibid.*, p. 45.

19 *Ibid.*

20 Max Lehrs, "Käthe Kollwitz," *Zukunft* (November 1903), p. 354.

21 Rowbotham, *Women*, p. 80.

22 Bebel, *Woman in the Past, Present and Future* (London: 1885), p. 113, quoted in Rowbotham, *Women*, p. 82.

23 Rowbotham, *Women*, p. 64.
24 Kollwitz, *Diary and Letters*, pp. 131–133.
25 Bonus-Jeep, *Sechzig Jahre*, p. 77.
26 *Ibid.*, p. 80.
27 *Ibid.*, pp. 89–90.
28 Kollwitz, *Diary and Letters*, p. 6.
29 Bonus-Jeep, *Sechzig Jahre*, pp. 87–88.
30 Kollwitz, *Diary and Letters*, p. 46.
31 *Ibid.*
32 *Ibid.*, p. 134. From a letter written by Kollwitz to her son Peter, dated June 10, 1907. While the letter is headed "Florence," the episode to which she refers probably occurred en route to Rome, since she dated her arrival in Rome as June 13, 1907.
33 *Ibid.*, p. 46.
34 *Ibid.*, p. 47.
35 *Ibid.*, p. 51.
36 *Ibid.*, p. 4.
37 *Ibid.*, p. 43.
38 Nagel, *The Drawings of Käthe Kollwitz*, p. 8.
39 Bonus-Jeep, *Sechzig Jahre*, p. 101.

# 6

## Seed for the planting must not be ground.

*Käthe twisted the lid* on the last canning jar with a firm wrench of her wrist, wiped her berry-stained hands with her apron, and placed the jar on a crowded shelf of homemade jams.

Hans announced, "The actors are ready!"

"Coming!" Käthe replied. She followed Lina into the living room and sat down on the "audience" couch.

Karl heard the clatter above him and climbed the stairs two at a time. He opened the apartment door to see the dining room table turned upside down in the hall. Carefully, he climbed over it and took his seat.

Käthe, Karl, Lina, Lise and her husband, Georg Stern, sat gazing at the "stage" before them. Old curtains and sheets formed the scenic background for the pagan goddesses and gods who were about to appear; and two chairs, one of them marked "Throne" stood waiting.

An "ahem" from behind the sheets cleared the air. The stirring in the audience stopped, though the giggling behind the curtain did not. Abruptly Hans pushed aside one of the clouds, walked to the center of the room, stood on one of the chairs, and, bowing low with a grand flourish, spoke.

Ladies and Gentlemen! We are proud to present to you—yes, the same company who performed the original *Siegfried and Gundhilda*, or *Treachery and*

111

*Loyalty*, Gorky's *Lower Depths*, and Shakespeare's *A Midsummer Night's Dream*, in which, by the way, some of the illustrious actors who took part now sit before me—yes, this same company is now happy to perform for you Schiller's *Semele!*

At *Semele* Hans stooped low in another bow, then jumped from the chair, accompanied by loud clapping.

For the next few hours Roman gods and goddesses, wrapped in togas created from bedsheets, made their entrances and exits in the earthly form of Peter, Hans, Georg (the child Käthe had brought from Paris) and Hanna and Rele Stern, Lise's oldest daughters. Toward the play's climax, Hans walked to the gas lamp on the wall, turned the wick knob up and down, and said with unquestioned omniscience, "Zeus alone can do this!"[1]

Käthe burst out laughing with the others. Pleased with the merriment he had elicited, Hans retreated backstage. He was especially pleased by his mother's hearty laughter, for he knew that she "longed for opportunities to laugh,"[2] even though, like Hans, she was not gifted in making others laugh.

All that was needed for these amateur theatricals was, in Käthe's opinion, a "capacity for enthusiasm."[3] She had possessed a great deal of this liveliness herself when she was younger, and now, as she watched her children, she delighted in observing it in them. This "capacity for enthusiasm" was the principal quality she wished her children to have.[4]

This capacity was also a "requirement" for family birthday celebrations, which often lasted all day. Hans' eighteenth birthday, celebrated in 1910, was typical of these joyous family occasions.

That morning, May 18, Käthe set out eighteen candles on the table, placing the tallest, the lifelight, in the center. Peter and Hans—now both taller than Käthe—stood with her and Karl around the table as Hans blew out the lifelight; then each read verses to him to mark the day.

Karl had to leave to open his clinic, but Käthe, Peter, Georg, and Hans went to Adami's Garden in Pankow Park, where Lise and her four daughters joined them; it was a family tradition to spend Hans' birthday there.

At four we went to Adami's. The weather was over-
cast, but very beautiful, the air damp and hot, the
apple trees in bloom. There was a thundershower
which we waited out in the hall; then, afterwards,
the delicious air. . . . In the evening we all went to
our house and had a bowl of punch.[5]

The folksong, "Lebe, Liebe" ("Live and love, drink,
rejoicing/ Wear a crown of gladness with me/ Grieve with me
when I am grieving/ And frolic with me when I'm merry"),
initiated the traditional family evening of song and dance. All
the members of both families—including Käthe's sons and Lise's
daughters—stood around in a circle singing "Lebe, Liebe,"
clinking their glasses with neighbors at every word until the
final note, when the one who "clinked" last had to step from
the circle.

By the end of this game they were all a bit tipsy, and the
celebrant, Hans, had been decorated with apple blossoms. Now
everyone was singing and dancing, including Käthe, who
danced alone or with her favorite partners—Hans on her left
and Peter on her right. They drank toasts, sang songs, recited
or read poems, and danced on and on. Käthe sang a favorite
East Prussian folk ballad; Hans recited a few lines from his
part in A Midsummer Night's Dream; and Käthe remembered
lines she had once spoken as Hermia. And, as always, Peter
made Käthe laugh at his good-natured antics.

The next day, Käthe thought about the party and the
growing sensuality—partly due, no doubt, to the punch—it had
revealed in her boys. She realized that her sons were boys no
more, but becoming men.

How strongly I feel that this is a dividing period in
their lives. How soon now something very real and
definite will emerge out of the boys' lovelorn
enthusiasms. Sensuality is burgeoning in all these
young people; it shows up in every one of their
movements, in everything, everything. It is only
a matter of opening a door and then they will understand it too, then the veil will be gone and the
struggle with the most powerful of instincts begin.
Never thereafter will they be entirely free of sen-

suality; often they will feel it their enemy, and sometimes they will almost suffocate for the joy it brings. Now all of them—Hans, Georg, Rele and Margret—are not yet quite awakened. I feel at once grave, ill at ease and happy as I watch our children—our *children*—growing to meet the greatest of instincts. May it have mercy on them![6]

Universal as these insights were, Käthe probably never shared them with her closest confidants, Lise, Jeep, or Karl. She did register them, however, in the journal she had started two years before, on September 18, 1908.

Why did she keep a journal? She offers no explanations herself. However, her personality and the types of entries she made over a period of thirty-four years suggest that the diary must have provided, along with her work, an important emotional outlet for her, of a kind not offered by her art. In the eleven books of her journal she drew only one sketch, a lightly penciled outline of *Tod, Frau und Kind* [Death, Woman, and Child], completed in 1910.

The journal allowed her to express to herself what she could not express to others. Her son Hans commented:

> Along with this reserve in talking about or showing love went a disinclination to speak about feelings at all, or about any personal matters. She could speak about other people and what happened to them, about books, about problems, even about her own works; but actually she never spoke about herself. This was consistent with the attitude which had prevailed in her grandparents' and parents' households: that one's work could be considered important, but oneself never. The same spirit underlies the inscription of the gravestone of her grandfather, Julius Rupp: "Man is not here to be happy, but to do his duty." To outsiders my mother gave the impression of being impregnable; only in her diaries can you see how she struggled with the antagonist within herself, and how essential that struggle was to her development.[7]

She was troubled that she vacillated between long months of depression and much shorter periods of productivity, and curious about the reasons. "Several times in her diaries she attempted to graph these periods and determine their course in advance."[8] But to no avail; she found no explanation for the rhythm—if there was one—of her creativity.

Käthe's relationship with Karl concerned her, and she recorded their growth as a couple from year to year. She also discussed intellectual, artistic, and moral questions, seeking answers to them. And, like all diarists, she wrote to preserve the quality of her life for its own sake.

The prose is high in literary quality, often poetic; the style is very readable. She wrote in a strong, flourishing hand, in black or dark blue ink, usually on unlined paper measuring seven by nine inches. She did not adhere to a predated schedule, but wrote freely until she had filled the pages of a volume, then began another; only the last book, that of 1943, is a predated diary. In the back of the first book, entered upside-down, is a financial list, apparently a record of payments for her work; yearly totals are recorded from 1901 to 1930, monthly accounts from 1908 to 1913. Until 1917 she wrote sporadically; after October of that year she made entries nearly every day.

One of Käthe's earliest entries reveals her increasing intimacy with poor women. The humiliating experience of her Aunt Yetta, who, years before, had been snubbed by Goethe's woman friend, Bettina von Armin, had stung her so deeply that she herself was unable to turn anyone away.

> Frau Pankopf was here. She had a bad black eye. Her husband had flown into a rage. When I asked her about him, she said he had wanted to be a teacher, but had become a worker in tortoise-shell and was well paid for his work. His heart became enlarged, and at the same time he had his first attack of extreme restlessness. He went for treatment and then tried to work again. It wouldn't do; he tried to get other work; and last winter went about with a hurdy-gurdy. His feet swelled, and the longer it went on the more he suffered from melancholy and nervousness. Wailed continually that he longed for death, could not support his family, and so on. . . .

The more I see of it, the more I realize that this is the *typical* misfortune of workers' families. As soon as the man drinks or is sick and unemployed, it is always the same story. Either he hangs on his family like a dead weight and lets them feed him—cursed by the other members of the family (Schwarzenau or Frank), or he becomes melancholy (Pankopf, Goenner), or he goes mad (likewise Frank), or he takes his own life. For the woman the misery is always the same. She keeps the children whom she must feed, scolds and complains about her husband. She sees only what has become of him and not how he became that way.[9]

In this entry Käthe speaks as a socialist, blaming the capitalist system for the workingman's condition and for the fact that the working-class woman is too busy—struggling to provide a life for those who depend upon her—to realize that capitalism, not her husband, is the cause of their problems. It was not feminism, but empathy, that drew her to these women, and they, in turn, to her.

As she became involved in their lives as a friend, more than as a neighbor, Käthe found the troubles of these people often too much for her to absorb. When this happened, her only recourse was to express her empathy and their suffering through her work.

*Überfahren* [Run Over], done this year, 1910, exemplifies this catharsis. This soft-ground etching is a scene of simultaneous horror and grief. A child, still in a baby gown, is carried by its father, who rushes ahead with a wide, determined stride. Behind him, the stricken mother supports the baby's head, almost touching it with her own as she bends in shock and grief. Her long, wide skirt flows with her rapid walking pace. Curious, excited, and terrified youngsters, their own and those of the neighborhood, surround the tragic couple, running along with them as they try to save the baby's life. Kollwitz, basically a dramatist, captures the tragedy at its peak, at the moment when the parents' emotions are raw with the sudden death. *Run Over* was one of the first pictures of a tragedy born out of the mass urbanization of the working class.

Käthe employed working-class women to model for her. One of her favorite models, with whom she became friends,

116

was the cheery, robust Frau Naujoks. In Frau Naujoks, as in Jeep and as in her son Peter, she was attracted to a personality more sanguine than her own. Modeling for a sculpture group of mother and child, Frau Naujoks inspired one of the few genuinely light-hearted works of Kollwitz' career. Käthe wrote of the woman:

> I am fond of her; she is loyal and good-natured. She totally supports her invalid husband. . . . She was splendid with the boy [model] when she held him on her lap and fooled with him. The boy was highly pleased with her nakedness; he behaved like a little animal, a young faun, with her. And she too was full of good-natured animal spirits. She has this non-sensical way of chattering with children which is just right for them.[10]

The outcome of this sitting was a 1910 etching, *Mutter mit Kind auf dem Arm* [Mother with Child in Arms], which shows the warm, happy touching of a mother and baby. Though Frau Naujoks inspired Käthe to catch the innocent joy of this picture, Käthe also drew upon her own special love for babies. Of all the periods of motherhood, the time when the child is newborn seemed the most lovely to her.

> I repeatedly dream that I again have a little baby, and I feel all the old tenderness again—or rather more than that, for all the feelings in a dream are intensified. What I have in these dreams is an inexpressibly sweet, lovely, physical feeling. First it was Peter who lay asleep, and when I uncovered him it was a very small baby exuding the warm bodily fragrance of babies.[11]

However, when Kollwitz identified *herself* with the mother figure in a graphic representing Mother and Child, Death entered the picture—as in *Tod und Frau* [Death and the Woman], completed the same year. The soft-ground etching is a masterpiece of line, space, and content. In its illustration of psychological tension through the drama of the body, *Death and the Woman* equals the artistry and emotional depth of Michelangelo's *Rebellious Slave*. A nude woman resembling the artist strains between a child who reaches for

*117*

her and the skeleton of Death, which grasps her, pinning back her arms. The child touches her breasts, but cannot reach her tormented face; neither is the mother able to wrench free of Death to touch her child. The woman is bound, crucifixlike, between Death and child, but in a dynamic pose: the line of her body curves powerfully from her right foot, through her taut thigh, to the near-circular arc of her breasts and her straining head, wrenched back in agony. The woman's left leg is angled, as if in running she had been caught between her child and Death. All major and supporting lines point to the woman's tortured face and to that of Death, which leers low behind her right shoulder.

With *Death and the Woman* Kollwitz had accomplished a technical goal she had set for herself the year before; in December, 1909, she had resolved that "I should like to do the new etching [very likely *Death and the Woman*] so that all the essentials are strongly stressed and the inessentials almost omitted."[12] Kollwitz had now perfected her etching technique so well that the broad lines and concentrated areas could easily be taken for a lithograph, even though it is the patient work of a meticulous etcher.

She repeated the same theme that year in a drawing and in an etching, both of them entitled *Frau, Tod, und Kind* [Woman, Death, and Child], but these portray passive, fathomless woe, rather than struggle. In the drawing, which is less harsh, the woman cradles the child's head breath-close to hers; her closed eyes, her nose, lips, and cheek press into his, and the two seem to float freely, gently, each into the other's being.

While Kollwitz was preoccupied with the subject of death, hers was not a morbid interest but rather an attempt to gain a more objective view of life, something she strove for in her private life as well as in her art. On September 29, 1910, she recorded in her journal:

> My wish is to die after Karl. I could endure living alone better than he could. I am also closer to the children. But if I should die Karl could not manage alone. If I die, Karl would find it unbearable by himself. He loves the children enough to die for them, and yet there is alienation between them. . . .

That is why Karl would be so unbearably alone if I should die before him. I know no person who can love as he can, with his whole soul. Often this love has oppressed me; I wanted to be free. But often too it has made me so terribly happy. I scarcely think I would ever leave him for very long.[13]

To many, the vision of *Death and the Woman*, and *Woman, Death, and Child* is harrowing, or oppressively sad. But it was the essentially tragic quality of life that gave Kollwitz her creative cutting edge; she appreciated joy, but the "joyous side simply did not appeal" to her as an artist.[14] Moreover, her awareness of the inevitability of death heightened the poignancy of her appreciation of life.

Wherever people love one another something very sad remains. Life remains always life to live, and so is earth-bound. Perhaps, for that very reason, life is all the more beautiful, for it is always permeated with this sadness. Why do tears run down people's faces just when they see the most basic, human sights? Because to become one with the earth is the most frightening reality.[15]

The specific source of her vision both in *Death and the Woman* and in *Woman, Death, and Child* is not clear, but it was an image—perhaps a premonition—that haunted her. She worried a great deal about her sons—their health and futures. Peter, with weak lungs, was prone to debilitating chest colds and other respiratory ailments; perhaps her constant worry about him prompted the fear of a child's death in her subconscious mind.

Ten years before, tuberculosis—one of the most common causes of death at this time—had taken Lisebeth Kollwitz, Karl's sister and Käthe's girlhood playmate. Her death caused Käthe and Karl to become even more solicitous about Peter's health. That winter, the boy had again fallen prey to a chest virus, and his racking cough had persisted. Käthe and Karl decided to take him out of school and put him in an expensive but good sanitorium for the rest of the winter.

In the period between leaving school and going to the spa, Peter had grown very bored at home and had requested watercolors for Christmas. Oddly enough, Käthe clearly considered this gift a luxury item for their tight budget; however, she bought him a set. She wrote to Jeep that during the winter he showed a great deal of interest in painting.

> He took the paints with him to the sanitorium and has brought back some sketches which I like very much. The boy sees colors and shows some things very nicely. I am really amazed at this, and secretly very happy about it. Maybe he can actually become a good painter. How good that would be! But maybe there will be other interests which will become greater than this one. Some years ago I was convinced that Peter would be a scientist, and, again, when I saw how he touched and treated our sick dog, I thought he would become a good doctor. So many qualities appear but you do not know which will last. His nature is somewhat lazy but he has a good sense of humor. I am not sure if he has the necessary strong will that it takes to become an artist.[16]

That spring all the Kollwitzes, and Lise's family, joined Peter in the mountains for a long hike. Inspired by her walking tour with Stan, Käthe, who "had a wonderful feeling for places,"[17] organized a trek through the snow-capped mountains and evergreen forests of Thuringia and Franconia, southwest of Berlin.

As usual, Käthe led the way. Behind her walked Lise, their husbands, their children, and Georg, all using *Alpenstöcke* ("metal walking sticks"). They had finished lunch on the mountain top and were slowly beginning to descend. Rele, Hanna, and Kati Stern usually sang as they hiked, but they were quiet now as they concentrated on following Aunt Käthe's steps down the treacherously steep, narrow path.

To Käthe's right was air; to the left, rock. Every step had to be planted carefully before the next.

Suddenly, a walking stick flew over Käthe's head, falling metal tip first, into the infinite hole of green air to her right, as if the hole were sucking it down. Its lightning speed terrified her. Whose was it. . . ? Would a body follow? Should she stop, turn around—scream? She wouldn't be able to stop the body. . . . Stop? No, impossible. Keep going, she decided.

At last she reached a few feet of flat ground and turned around. Incredibly, everyone was there, chatting enthusiastically about the perilous climb.

"Did you see my walking stick?" Peter asked Käthe. "I'm glad it didn't get in between your feet."

Käthe, too shocked to answer, said, under her breath, "It has killed me anyway."[18]

At home, her creative spirit was restless. She now desired only the essentials, so successfully isolated in the soft-ground, *Death and the Woman*. But etching, even her perfected technique of soft ground, was losing its appeal to her as a medium of expression.

Perhaps inevitably, Kollwitz had recently begun to explore the possibilities of working in stone and clay. She had no training in sculpture, and she did not know whether she would be able to produce any work of quality; even so, she continued to experiment and to learn the medium's physical and aesthetic properties.

She visited Berlin's Old Museum, which she called *Die Grossen* [The Great Ones] and the National Gallery, seeking the stimulation of the work there. While at the National Gallery, admiring the color sense of some contemporary French painters, she happened to hear a conversation between a museum attendant and a young woman painter.

> I suddenly realized that they were talking about me, and the museum attendant was praising my work to the sky. But he had no backbone, for when the painter took issue with him, he became more and more timid, and finally said, "Yes, that's so, of course; women ought to stick to their households."[19]

As many critics have noted, Kollwitz possessed a marked bent for sculpture. One plan, the original conception of which was unfortunately never realized (or was perhaps destroyed), reflects her growing sensitivity to the special forms and messages that could be achieved in sculpture.

> I imagine the following sculpture as utterly beautiful: a pregnant woman chiseled out of stone. Carved

*121*

> only down to the knees so that she looks the way
> Lise said she did the time she was pregnant with
> Maria: "As if I am rooted to the ground." The
> immobility, restraint, introspection. The arms and
> hands dangling heavily, the head lowered, all atten-
> tion directed inward. And the whole thing in heavy,
> heavy stone. Title: *Pregnancy.*[20]

Käthe's own maternal relationship to her family was changing radically. Now her sons left home for increasingly longer stays. At present, Hans was a student at the University of Freiburg, in the southwest, near the edge of the Black Forest. He had wished to become an actor, but many actors— and Karl as well—had advised him against entering such an economically unstable profession. Peter was in the east, a farmhand in the fields of Poland, smoking the farmhands' pungent tobacco and learning their lively dialect, curses, and tales.

For the first time since she had been a student, Käthe had a great deal of free time. "Aunt Lina," as always, helped her and, from time to time, two younger women helped Lina with the work of the Kollwitz household. Kollwitz spent the majority of her time in her studio, at work on sculpture.

> I am gradually approaching the period in my life
> when work comes first. When both the boys went
> away for Easter, I hardly did anything but work.
> Worked, slept, ate and went for short walks. But
> above all I worked. And yet I wonder whether the
> "blessing" is not missing from such work. No
> longer diverted by other emotions, I work the way
> a cow grazes; but Heller once said that such calm is
> death. Perhaps in reality I "accomplish" little
> more.[21]

For many years she had looked forward to this time when she would be free of the responsibility of Hans and Peter, and many times she had discussed it with Jeep. The two old friends even had a fantasy—decipherable only to them—about this time, which they referred to as their "deer age" when, no longer responsible for rearing children—or, in this case, fawns— they would acquire all the characteristics of the buck—his commanding antlers and great physical strength, but above all his freedom, a freedom in which they could live as they pleased. Actually, Käthe had dreamed of living and working in Paris, once Karl and the children no longer needed her.

> . . . but from year to year it becomes more and more questionable when the time will come when I will be free. Sometimes the whole idea seems like an illusion. Once you have lived together for twenty years it is not easy to declare one day that now you want to go your own way. By the way, though, I must say that I am glad that my family still needs me. When this is no longer the case I am afraid I will be existing in a kind of ice age.[22]

For years she had planned on this free time. But now that it had arrived, Käthe had neither the physical and mental strength, nor the need, to enjoy it alone. She was growing older; her hair shone prematurely silver. She never did visit Paris, although her work did.

Menopause—or her expectations about it—affected her personality and work even more dramatically than did aging. For the first time in her career, due to irregular menstrual periods, she experienced immobilizing insecurity about her work. The irregularity unsettled her, and she railed against it. She recorded in her log:

> This is the second time I have destroyed work which required weeks to create. I felt almost driven to do this when I got my period and didn't know or expect I was getting it. The next day I found that menstruation had been the reason for my destructiveness. I and probably most women suffer similar pathological pressure during menstruation.[23]

She was used to obeying her will rather than her body; now she was being buffeted by the disconcerting up-and-down moods of menopause.

She feared that the changes in her body would sap her physical energy to the point of ending her creativity. A deadening mood of futility and depression overwhelmed her. Nothing engaged her usually alert intellect and social conscience for a significant period of time. It was a damaging time, fraught with anxiety. When she saw her physician, Dr. Krause, he took Xrays, and she gathered that she would probably have to undergo an operation—perhaps a hysterectomy.

> I am afraid of the operation without anesthesia and I am worried about what these important changes will do to my body. Becoming sterile and, in addition, taking out my thyroid gland? What will remain of myself other than the mother and Karl's wife? For a long time now I have had the feeling that it is not worth it any more. I have said what I had to say and the rest is unimportant. . . . Beneath all the stirring plans and activities, especially the sculpture, but also the trip to Russia and London, is the feeling it is not worth it any more. But I am not even fifty years old. I could count on at least ten more years of consistent working ability. But the deep faith within myself is lacking.[24]

This passage in her diary indicated Käthe's return to the myth that "biology is destiny," a belief she had categorically rejected from the time she was a student. Now, the possibility that she might have to undergo a hysterectomy prompted her to doubt her artistic strength—what she referred to as "potency"[25]—for the first time. She believed that her sexuality, manifested in her ability to produce children, also positively influenced her artistic creativity. It is not surprising that she believed this, for men, dominant in art, had equated the two for centuries; of course, this theory assumed that the artist was male. Because Kollwitz believed that the "masculine" element within her helped her to create, and thus identified to some extent with men (or at least with the male psyche), it is understandable that she adopted some of their views in order to understand herself.

When she was younger and had more physical energy, it had been easier to rebel against the idea of biology as destiny; now, in her mid-forties, her body older, Käthe succumbed to the myth and its accompanying inhibitions. The self-portraits of these years reflect her doubt and fatigue. Technically, they are excellent studies; psychologically, they reflect a wearying woman of middle age. Except in a few instances, the artist does not look out at us with bold self-assurance; one eye is consistently hidden in shadow. In one portrait, a drawing dated 1911, she appears racked with pain, the light around her head and arms giving her an aura of frenzy, creating an image of contained hysteria.

Her diary, too, registered ambiguity. In March, 1911, she thoroughly blacked out half a page with heavy ink. At the end of 1911 she wrote a brief survey of the year:

> ...What about myself? Summing up of 1911? Progress? No progress in my relationship with Karl. What he always speaks of, what seems to him still the sole worthwhile goal of our long living together— that we should grow together in the deepest intimacy—I still do not feel and probably never will learn to feel.
>
> Are not the ties with the boys also growing slacker? I almost think so. For the last third of life there remains only work. It alone is always stimulating, rejuvenating, exciting and satisfying.[26]

During these years Germany was no less turbulent than the artist. Divided within, "The Fatherland" was about to be divided from much of Europe by war.

The rise of nationalism throughout Europe was given an especially unfortunate emphasis in the Germany of this time through the belligerent, authoritarian personality of Kaiser Wilhelm II. The Kaiser's aggressive military posture was supported by the land-owing Junkers (the officer class of the military) and by the bankers and industrialists. The interests of these groups were also served, domestically, by a monarchy unhampered by democratic or constitutional restraints.

In 1912 there were still many who opposed these forces, as evidenced by the enormous victories scored in that year's national elections by the Social Democratic Party. Together with the Radical and the National Liberal parties, it polled two-thirds of twelve million votes. The new Reichstag, however, still hemmed about by royal prerogatives and limited severely in its political power, was virtually impotent. "The Prussian bastion of royalism was unconquerable for the opposition."[27]

(text continued on page 130)

PLATE 13. *Tod und Frau* [Death and the Woman] , 1910, etching and sandpaper soft ground.

PLATE 14. *Arbeiterfrau mit Ohrring* [Working Woman with Earring],
1910, etching.

PLATE 15. *Nude Study: Working Woman*, 1910–12, drawing, charcoal and pencil.

PLATE 16. *Nude Study: Working Woman*, 1910–12, drawing, charcoal and pencil.

The Kaiser's anachronistic belief in the divine right of kings, his touting of the military virtues of "courage, honor and unconditional blind obedience,"[28] his contempt for civilian rule were readily subscribed to by those who feared the social unrest that lay below the surface of German wealth and power. The effect of the show of antimonarchical strength in the 1912 elections was to drive the government further into the arms of the right.[29] A period of repression set in, during which, according to one political analyst, "only men of the greatest independence dare to utter their convictions openly."[30]

Yet Kollwitz, a woman, spoke out—at this point on a poster illustrating the miserable housing of poor Berliners. In *Für Gross Berlin* [For Greater Berlin], a young girl stands holding a baby in her arms. A sign, *Spielen verboten* ("Playing in the Yard is Forbidden"), hangs on a drab tenement wall behind her. The lithographed poster announced a free public meeting to air the housing grievances of workers. Kollwitz used bold, black letters to state that

> 600,000 Berliners live in apartments in which five or more persons are living. Some hundred thousand children live in tenement housing without playgrounds.

Shortly after *Für Gross Berlin* was posted on buildings and billboards, the Kaiser—who had repeatedly denounced Kollwitz' work as "art of the gutter"—ordered it removed on the grounds that it incited class hatred.

In these unfortunate times, the 1848 Revolution was venerated by progressives as a signal event in German history, for it had sought to achieve socialism and unity among German-speaking peoples. Its date, March 18, had now become a day of mourning observed by thousands of workers.

Twenty-five years earlier, Kollwitz had paid tribute to the March Dead along with Konrad. This year she was one of thousands. Police guarded the cemetery entrance, sometimes confiscating commemorative Marxist banners. Wreaths and red banners decked the stones, especially the grave of the unknown soldier. It was a solemn procession, and Kollwitz, in her 1913 lithograph, *Märzfriedhof* [Graves of the Victims of the 1848

Revolution, The March Cemetery], pictured the scene with a few, strong, broad strokes—almost outlines—accenting the workers' large, expressive hands and pensive faces as they mourned the dead revolutionaries.

The Secession responded to the times by tightening its structure as a mutually protective band of artists. Since its start in the 1890's, the group had grown to signify the best in European art, but because of a wave of conservatism within the organization, a new Secession had been formed in 1910. Now, out of a roster of 228 (including non-Berliners), twelve women were listed—among them such strikingly gifted young artists as Emy Roeder and Renée Sintenis. *Die Neue Sezession* show of 1910 took up ten large rooms in a building at 208/7 Kurfürstendamm, on Berlin's great avenue, and included works by Klee, Kandinsky, Gauguin, Manet, and the innovative German colorist Paula Modersohn-Becker.

While the Berlin-based New Secession now numbered a few outstanding women among its members, the position of women members remained marginal. In a revealing letter to Hans, written in February, 1913, Kollwitz described her professional status among her colleagues.

> . . . These days there is one Secession meeting after the other. And I really have not escaped my destiny; they've saddled me with a horrible job, that of second secretary. Which means that when Baluschek is absent I have to take minutes, and so on. I protested that I couldn't do it, but Cassirer said I ought to try and if I really couldn't they would replace me. And so I now have that on my back. To give you an idea of how much this job has disturbed me: the following night I dreamed that the Secession had given me the task of pasting a quantity of red stickers on the advertising columns. With a pail of paste hanging at my belt and a large brush, I ran breathlessly from column to column, pasting on my red stickers and trembling for fear I was doing it wrong. . . .
>
> If only the Secession board, instead of making me secretary would send me to Duesseldorf to arrange the exhibition affairs there.[31]

That she had been elected second secretary, and not a juror, humiliated her, not so much because of the position itself, but because of its demeaning social status: she had been elected secretary because of her sex, not for her artistic merit. As this passage clearly shows, the job degraded her, in her own eyes as well as in those of her colleagues, and she hated it.

In 1913 the Reichstag acceded to the Kaiser's call for a giant allocation of funds to the army. On June 28, 1914, the assassination of Archduke Ferdinand, successor to the Hapsburg throne, triggered the rapid series of events that, by the first days of August, had plunged Europe into the tragedy of the First World War. The SPD, motivated in part by enmity to czarist Russia, in part by the legal and political untenability of an antiwar position, joined in the unanimous parliamentary vote for war funds. In the holocaust that followed, socialists of one nation fought socialists of another, all in the name of the defense of their homelands.

At the beginning of August, Käthe and Karl were in Königsberg for a visit with relatives. From their hotel room they heard soldiers singing marching songs on their way to the depot. Karl ran to the streets to see them pass, but Käthe, devastated, "sat on the bed and wept, wept, wept."[32]

What she called the "heroic stiffness" of wartime, "when our feelings are screwed to an unnatural pitch," bewildered her.[33] She was overcome by melancholy.[34]

Three weeks after the war broke out, she read an article by Gabriel Reuter in the *Tag* [The Daily] on the task of women.

> She spoke of the joy of sacrificing—a phrase that struck me hard. Where do all the women who have watched so carefully over the lives of their beloved ones get the heroism to send them to face the cannon? I am afraid that this soaring of the spirit will be followed by the blackest despair and dejection. The task is to bear it not only during these few weeks, but for a long time—in dreary November as well, and also when spring comes again, in March, the month of young men who wanted to live and are dead. That will be much harder. . . . For us, whose sons are going, the vital thread is snapped.[35]

Wartime speeded up old jobs and created new ones. As usual, Karl was booked heavily with patients. Hans, infused with Germanic chauvinism, had joined the army and was training in one of the many Berlin platoon barracks. Käthe went to work as a cook and cafeteria helper, feeding large numbers of the unemployed, especially destitute mothers and children.

Peter, too, wanted to offer himself to his country's defense. His parents tried to dissuade him from volunteering. Like many others, Käthe and Karl expected a swift end to the war; they pointed out to Peter—who was just eighteen— that when the war ended, young people would be needed to rebuild the Fatherland. But Peter, like many of his peers, was "imbued with Hoelderlin's conception of 'death for the Fatherland' and with the idea of sacrifice."[36] Finally, after hours of frustrating discussion, they agreed to let him volunteer.

Peter entered the infantry at Prenzlau, about sixty miles north of Berlin. Because of poor connections, the trip took over four hours each way. Käthe visited him twice a week, and Karl once each Sunday. After dinner they went together to see Hans in the city barracks.

Käthe did no artistic work during this period, and kept water on her semimodeled clay so that it would not dry out. Feeling that her art was not as important as feeding children, she spent most of her working day trying to meet their urgent needs. Like the majority of Germans at the outset of the war, Käthe believed that the strength and effort of the individual belonged to the Fatherland. Her son Hans wrote that her early melancholy was for a time swept away "by the attitude of the young men, and especially by the enthusiasm of my brother Peter and his friends," and that only later did she come to embrace a pacifist position.[37]

Even at the beginning, however, her feelings were mixed; she found the war repugnant and its demands upon her as a mother impossible to accept. On September 30, 1914, she wrote in her diary:

> Nothing is real but the frightfulness of this state, which we almost grow used to. In such times it

seems so stupid that the boys must go to war. The whole thing is so ghastly and insane. Occasionally there comes the foolish thought: how can they possibly take part in such madness? And at once the cold shower: they *must, must*! All is leveled by death; down with all the youth! Then one is ready to despair.

Only one state of mind makes it all bearable; to receive the sacrifice into one's will. But how can one maintain such a state?[38]

She had not found an answer, nor had her questioning prepared her for the news received a few weeks later from a family friend, Walter Koch: Peter had been killed in Belgium. Käthe fell to the depths of grief, never to fully recover.

Slowly, as the weeks passed, Käthe began to find her way to consolation. She responded to Peter's death with life—her life as an artist. She now sought inspiration for her work from Peter. In what can only be described as prayers to him, she summoned his presence to help her in her work. On New Year's Eve, 1914, she wrote the following:

My Peter, I intend to try to be faithful.... What does that mean? To love my country in my own way as you loved it in your way. And to make this love work. To look at the young people and be faithful to them. Besides that I shall do my work, the same work, my child, which you were denied. I want to honor God in my work, too, which means I want to be honest, true, and sincere.... When I try to be like that, dear Peter, I ask you then to be around me, help me, show yourself to me. I know you are there, but I see you only vaguely, as if you were shrouded in mist. Stay with me.... my love is different from the one which cries and worries and yearns.... But I pray that I can feel you so close to me that I will be able to make your spirit live in my work.[39]

She felt, at first, that keeping faith with her son, who had given his life as a voluntary sacrifice, meant that she, too, should be willing to sacrifice her life.[40] She wished that it had been her life, not his, that had been sacrificed. After months of agony, she arrived at a resolution. She found in Goethe's *Saatfrüchte sollen nicht vermahlen werden* ("seed for the planting must not be ground") the moral, philosophic, and emotional basis she needed, as a mother and an artist, to continue living and working.

> I do not want to die, even if Hans and Karl should die. I do not want to go until I have faithfully made the most of my talent and cultivated the seed that was placed in me until the last small twig has grown. This does not contradict the fact that I would have died—smilingly—for Peter, and for Hans too, were the choice offered me. Oh how gladly, how gladly. Peter was seed for the planting which should not have been ground. He was the sowing. I am the bearer and cultivator of a grain of seed-corn. What Hans will become, the future will show. But since I am to be the cultivator, I want to serve faithfully. Since recognizing that, I am almost serene and much firmer in spirit. It is not only that I am permitted to finish my work—I am obliged to finish it. This seems to me to be the meaning of all the gabble about culture. Culture arises only when the individual fulfills his cycle of obligations. If everyone recognizes and fulfills his cycle of obligations, genuineness emerges. The culture of a whole nation can in the final analysis be built upon nothing else but this.[41]

She attached to "seed for the planting must not be ground" a complex of complementary meanings and feelings. The first and most important meaning related to Peter's untimely death in war: he should have lived so that his seed of life and talent would have borne fruit. As a result of his death, she gradually reversed her position on this war, and all war, affirming that there was no justification for Peter—or for any of the young volunteers, of whatever country—to have been "seed for planting" in the bloody fields of war.

In a less dramatic sense her talent was also "seed for planting" not to be ground. In order to fulfill her promise to Peter, she had to continue cultivating the seed of talent growing within her.

*135*

There was yet another aspect. Shortly after his eighteenth birthday, Peter had decided that he wanted to continue his art lessons and become a painter, despite his mother's warning that he had "chosen to walk on the bumpiest sort of corduroy road."[42] She grieved that Peter would never be able to give his artistic gifts to the world. Her renewed dedication to her work was in part her attempt to carry forward the contribution Peter might have made. In the winter following Peter's death, she turned to concrete plans.

Up to this time, Kollwitz's art had risen from emotional needs for self-expression, from the aesthetic impulse, and, later, from a sophisticated social conscience. Now she committed herself to an almost religious vow to create *for Peter.* "Seed for the planting must not be ground" became her imperative. Her resolve to be true to its meanings perhaps saved her life; certainly, it made it possible for her to take up her work and her life again affirmatively.

Kollwitz conceived of a memorial sculpture dedicated to Peter and to all the young volunteers who had sacrificed their lives. She felt that "no one has more right than I to make this memorial."[43]

Unfortunately, she found that designing the memorial was an easier task than executing it, for her emotional intensity often crippled her efforts. As a mourning mother she was as yet unable to make her deep private suffering public. As an artist, however, she was obliged, ultimately, to reveal her emotions—as she always had—before the eyes of strangers. As she began work on Peter's memorial, she experienced great conflict between her "self-expressive" self and her "objective" self. The following passage describes this trial, reflecting the struggle, rather than the harmony, between her "masculine" and "feminine" selves: the vulnerability, the intense feeling, the passion are there, but so overwhelming that she is unable to objectify and create a work in which passion is controlled by skill.

> Stagnation in my work.
>
> When I feel so parched, I almost long for the sorrow again. And then when it comes back I feel it stripping me physically of all the strength I need for work.

Made a drawing: the mother letting her dead son slide into her arms. I might make a hundred such drawings and yet I do not get any closer to him. I am seeking him. As if I had to find him in the work. And yet everything I can do is so childishly feeble and inadequate. I feel obscurely that I could throw off this inadequacy, that Peter is somewhere in the work and I might find him. And at the same time I have the feeling that I can no longer do it. I am too shattered, weakened, drained by tears. I am like the writer in Thomas Mann: he can only write, but he has not sufficient strength to live what is written. It is the other way round with me. I no longer have the strength to form what has been lived. A genius and a Mann could do it. I probably cannot.

For work, one must be hard and thrust outside oneself what one has lived through. As soon as I begin to do that, I again feel myself a mother who will not give up her sorrow. Sometimes it all becomes so terribly difficult.[44]

Slowly Kollwitz worked on Peter's memorial, sometimes in concert with herself, sometimes in battle. She turned again to her most effortless skill, drawing, and in 1916 produced one self-study. It was a close-up—the mouth, nose, and eyes gently shaded and the details, even outlines, of hair, ears, and neck omitted. The artist turns to the left as she gazes long and hard into the well of suffering within.

A self-portrait at this time was a Herculean task for Kollwitz, but she accomplished it with a rare and sublime beauty. She maintained that "It always comes back to this: that only one's inner feelings represent the truth;"[45] and this study, her first after Peter's death, once again displays her amazing ability to unmask her soul. The work's soft texture together with its harsh inner reality are striking; it is one of the most widely published of her self-portraits.

With this quarter-profile, Käthe began to resume her graphic work. She repeated the happy classic of Frau Naujoks and baby as a lithograph, *Mother Holding Child in Arms*, and this version is much warmer and more flowing than the earlier etching.

In 1916 she also drew *Angst. Die Witwe* [Anguish. The Widow], in which a pregnant working-class woman, gaunt and harried, stands nearly full-length before us; her large-knuckled hands, cupped to hold and embrace, reach out limply in empty space. The woman is shocked and despondent from mourning; the woman is Kollwitz, who felt the widow's grief through the loss of her own son; the poor woman's desolation is her own.

> ... Where are my children now? What is left to their mother? One boy to the right and one to the left, my right son and my left son, as they called themselves. One dead and one so far away [at the front], and I cannot help him, cannot give to him out of myself. All has changed forever. Changed, and I am impoverished. My whole life as a mother is really behind me now. I often have a terrible longing to have it back again—to have children, my boys, one to the right and one to the left; to dance with them as formerly when spring arrived and Peter came with flowers and we danced a springtide dance.[46]

In the last year Karl had grown more precious to her. "Karl and I are now growing more and more intimately used to one another. What life did not accomplish up to a year ago, this year has accomplished."[47] That June, on their silver wedding anniversary, she expressed her feelings toward him in an uncharacteristic outpouring.

> I have never been without your love, and because of it we are now so firmly linked after twenty-five years. Karl, my dear, thank you. I have so rarely told you in words what you have been and are to me. Today I want to do so, this once. I thank you for all you have given me out of your love and kindness. The tree of our marriage has grown slowly, somewhat crookedly, often with difficulty. But it has not perished. The slender seedling has become a tree after all, and it is healthy at the core. It bore two lovely, supremely beautiful fruits.
>
> From the bottom of my heart I am thankful to the fate which gave us our children and in them such inexpressible happiness.

138

If Hans is let live, we shall be able to see his further development, and perhaps we may expect children of his. If he too is taken, then all the sunlight that out of him lighted, warmed and made everything golden will be smothered; but we shall still hold tight to one another's hands to the end, and remain heart to heart.[48]

Grateful as she was for Karl's strength and love, it could not fulfill her. Only her work could do that. And now, in the outside world, there were artistic developments that interested her.

A new aesthetic theory, "expressionism," engaged her contemporaries. Two groups of artists, *Der Blaue Reiter* ("The Blue Rider"), formed in 1911 in Munich by Franz Marc and Wassily Kandinsky, and *Die Brücke* ("The Bridge"), organized in 1905 in Dresden by Ernst Ludwig Kirchner, Erich Heckel, and Karl Schmidt-Rottluff, had helped form the current expressionist movement. Although *Der Blaue Reiter*—most of whom were painters—had no dominant style, most of its adherents subscribed to the principle that art should discard external realities in favor of the expression of the artist's inner—spiritual, psychological, or emotional—truths. The artists of *Die Brücke*, very much alive to a complex of modern literary and political influences, were also inspired by the old Germanic tradition of woodcut, especially as extended and elaborated in the masterly work of Dürer. While Kollwitz never joined *Die Brücke*, her work, too, was strongly nourished by the German graphic tradition, and she shared *Die Brücke* artists' use of the human image to express psychological and social realities. By this year, 1916, the two groups had dissolved, and expressionism—fundamentally understood as the expression of the primacy of the artist's "inner life" over that of the technical form—now absorbed former advocates of these groups, as well as the majority of Kollwitz' colleagues.

As the war continued, and more and more artists became disaffected, the term "expressionism" in Germany came to be used broadly to apply to any artist holding nonestablishment sociopolitical views and working in a nonformalist style. Because of this broad definition, and because of her own

*139*

marked inclination toward self-expression, Kollwitz was often mistakenly called an expressionist. In fact, however, Kollwitz sometimes found herself opposed to expressionism as "pure studio art." Within her circle of prominent German artists, she was one of the few who never gave allegiance to any purely expressionist group or doctrine. As the following diary entry indicates, it was often disheartening for her to battle against these artistic "odds." On March 31, 1916, she wrote,

> I am overcome by a terrible depression. Gradually I am realizing the extent to which I already belong among the old fogies, and my future lies behind me. Now I am looked upon more or less kindly as a dignitary. If I had less of a name I would be treated like Loewenstein and Siewert; I would be rejected.[49]

The expressionist movement forced her to grapple with her identity and integrity as an artist. This confrontation made her decide to "return, without illusions, to what there is in me and go on working very quietly. Go on with my work to its end."[50]

Throughout her life she had sought to be free of everything that obfuscated her true self. Every artist tends toward self-expression, but Kollwitz used this unusually strong tendency in herself to examine and/or resolve personal conflicts and truths. Whether as art student, wife and mother, revolutionary, adventurer, or very private artist, she regarded her work as an avenue of self-discovery. Not only did she follow her feelings; she acted upon them with conviction, for in her singular quest she often disagreed with her colleagues and her society. Thus, she was often a loner in her art.

Although her university training (briefer than and presumably inferior to the instruction received by her male counterparts in the larger, more substantial Academy) had emphasized realism, Kollwitz did not classify herself as a realist. Rather, as she had done with naturalism, she used some aspects of realism, finally transcending it to form *her* style. "To Kollwitz 'realism' was not a style; rather, it was . . . a matter of the genuineness of communication. . . . Kollwitz defended that art which could communicate to people without compromising its content, its message, its power or its form"[51] Kollwitz described some of the complexities of this position in a 1916 journal entry:

> E. von Keyserling ... opposes expressionism and says that after the war the German people will need eccentric studio art less than ever before. What they need is realistic art.
>
> I quite agree—if by realistic art Keyserling means the same thing I do. . . .
>
> . . . Art for the average spectator need not be shallow. Of course he has no objection to the trite— but it is also true that he would accept true art if it were simple enough. I thoroughly agree that there must be understanding between the artist and the people. In the best ages of art that has always been the case.
>
> Genius can probably run on ahead and seek out new ways. But the good artists who follow after genius— and I count myself among these—have to restore the lost connection once more. A pure studio art is unfruitful and frail, for anything that does not form living roots—why should it exist at all?
>
> Now as for myself. The fact that I am getting too far away from the average spectator is a danger to me. I am losing touch with him. I am groping in my art, and who knows, I may find what I seek. When I thought about my work at New Year's 1914, I vowed to myself and to Peter that I would be more scrupulous than ever in "giving the honor to God, that is, in being wholly genuine and sincere." Not that I felt myself drifting away from sincerity. But in groping for the precious truth one falls easily into artistic oversubtleties and ingenuities—into preciosity. I suddenly see that very clearly, and I must watch out. Perhaps the work on the memorial will bring me back to simplicity.[52]

Beginning with her student days, Kollwitz had tried to foster this rapport between artist and people by choosing etching as her medium, so that as many prints as possible could be distributed to the working class. She preferred a

(*text continued on page 146*)

PLATE 17. Käthe Kollwitz.

PLATE 18. Käthe Kollwitz.

PLATE 19. Käthe Kollwitz.

144

PLATE 20. Käthe Kollwitz.

democratic price range, too. A single print cost approximately fifteen to thirty marks (two to six dollars). She never earned a great deal of money from her work.

In 1916, three years after being elected to the despised secretarial post, Kollwitz was voted the first woman juror of the New Secession. She was awarded the position on her merits as much as on the basis of tokenism. Possibly also, her colleagues thought that the added responsibilities of being a juror would help to take her mind off Peter.

Even in her privileged position as a woman within the New Secession—indeed, as one of the few well-known women artists in Europe—she never underestimated the difficulties encountered by other women artists. She recalled her own struggles too well to deny the importance of any artistic work done by a woman. However, now that she had succeeded in gaining the esteemed position of juror, she found the post an awkward one for her. As a woman with a strong feminist perspective, she wanted to encourage and support women and their work; but as an artist she had developed certain critical standards that sometimes made it impossible for her to be an enthusiastic champion. In her log she confessed:

> My unpleasant position on the jury. I always find myself forced to defend the cause of a woman. But because I can never really do that with conviction, since most of the work in question is mediocre (if the works are better than that the other jury members will agree), I always become involved in equivocations.[53]

As this passage indirectly indicates, some of Kollwitz' female colleagues were producing work that was *not* mediocre; besides the New Secession artists already mentioned, there were Gabriele Münter, Martha Schrag, Clara Westhoff, Milly Steger, Chana Orlowa. While Kollwitz was foremost, and almost alone in surviving subsequent exclusion by art historians, these women and others shared and contributed to the cultural ferment of early-twentieth-century Germany.

Cassirer's Gallery, in central Berlin, was the focal point of most Secessionist activity, including antiwar events. Now, as the war created increasing despair, Cassirer's held an antiwar poetry reading. Despite ruthless repression, the underground antiwar movement—initiated with the SPD's rejection of the war budget in March, 1913—was a growing force.

Kollwitz was devoted to modern poetry; one of her favorite activities—along with hiking and listening to classical music—was reading and listening to poetry; indeed, she preferred modern poetry to modern painting. She attended the "invitation only" poetry reading at Cassirer's and gave a moving account of it in a letter that Hans received in February, 1917, at the front, where he was serving as a medical noncombatant.

> ... Madame Durieux read a story by Leonhard Frank: *The Waiter.* In 1894 an only son is born to a waiter. The old story of working solely for the sake of this child. The son goes to secondary school, is planning to go on to the university. Then comes the war. The son falls. The father receives the slip of paper with the familiar words. "On the field of honor" seems to him a phrase out of a foreign language. Work becomes meaningless to him; he falls more and more to brooding. And then, one day while he is waiting on the guests at a trade-union dinner, or something of the sort, he finds speech. He begins to talk, to clothe in stammering words his horror of the war. The people, all of whom have been struck hard by the war, grasp his meaning. A wave of excitement goes through them. As a body they leave the restaurant; others outside join them. Soon there is a procession, a stormy group of people carried along by passion. Someone cries, "Peace!" and the cry is taken up. A vast shout for peace fills the street. Madame Durieux read this with mounting passion and excitement of her own. It was almost unendurable. I could scarcely keep control of myself, and I felt that I was not the only one. When she had finished and her last word, "Peace," faded away, someone in the audience called out aloud, as though overpowered by a tremendous emotion: "Peace, Peace," again and again. It was as if we were all swept up on the same wave.[54]

That summer Cassirer's commemorated Käthe's fiftieth birthday with a retrospective. Few artists enjoy retrospective shows in their lifetime, or, in the event of one, such wide critical acclaim. The exhibit of her life's work, from age seventeen to age fifty, met with resounding praise. The display of over fifty drawings, many of which were shown publicly for the first time, formed a separate but accomplished *oeuvre*. As critic Willy Kurth noted, the drawings demonstrated a technical excellence as well as an emotional spontaneity that was sometimes lost in the transferred lines of the etching and lithographs.[55] Because the reviewers knew her personally, and because she feared that they might be overly sympathetic to her work on account of the loss of Peter, she was doubtful about its acclaim. She still underestimated the instinctive truth of her art.

> I can scarcely think that I have been *so* able to communicate myself or—more than that—to have been the direct mediator between people and something they are not conscious of, something transcendent, primal.[56]

Of all the critical reviews of her work, Kollwitz most appreciated Lise's, printed in the May, 1917 issue of *Monatsheft*, a socialist monthly. She wrote of this article written by her sister:

> She makes a point which is for the most part ignored when people assert that my one subject is always the lot of the unfortunate. Sorrow isn't confined to social misery. All my work hides within it *life itself*, and it is with life that I contend through my work. It is difficult to express oneself clearly about one's work. At any rate I felt that Lise's conception is very close to mine. Which is after all natural.[57]

The overwhelming favorable response to her show surprised, and, at the same time, humbled her.

> From so many sides I am being told that my work has value, that I have accomplished something, wielded influence. This echo of one's life work is *very* good; it is satisfying and produces a feeling of gratitude. And of self-assurance as well. But at the age of fifty this kind of self-assurance is not as

excessive and arrogant as it is at thirty. It is based upon self-knowledge. One knows best oneself where one's own upper and lower limits are. The word fame is no longer intoxicating.

But it might have turned out differently. In spite of all the work I have done, success might have been denied me. There was an element of luck in it, too. And certainly I am grateful that it has turned out this way.[58]

Käthe was now highly motivated to work. Day after day, without tiring, she worked on Peter's memorial. "I have the feeling that I am on the right track. Like running along behind someone you have not yet caught, but you know you can keep him in sight, you are at his heels."[59] The memorial changed from a sculpture of Peter to a relief of mourning parents—herself and Karl: a monumental headstone for the entire cemetery where Peter lay. From the time that she changed the memorial from the shape of Peter to the relief of the parents, she would not permit Karl to see it.

In size and in spiritual, emotional, and physical energy, this was the largest work Kollwitz had ever planned; and she resigned herself to the years of work which would be required for its completion. Constantly, she strove for greater simplicity, to distill the human form to its most basic, expressive features and lines. "As always only the total attitude and the face and hands speak to me."[60] All her working time was concentrated on the memorial, and she often prayed that she would not grow old and infirm before she finished it.

She longed to be relieved of the war and its constant toll of death and despair. She sought a lighter, more hopeful mood to lift the oppressive weight of the war; but such release was not to be found.

How can one cherish joy now when there is really nothing that gives joy? And yet the imperative is surely right. For joy is really equivalent to strength. It is possible to have joy within oneself and yet shoulder all the suffering. Or is it really impossible?

If all the people who have been hurt by the war were to exclude joy from their lives, it would almost be as if they had died. Men without joy seem like corpses. They seem to obstruct life. . . . When someone dies because he has been sick—even if he is still young—the event is so utterly beyond one's power that one *must* gradually become resigned to it. He is dead because it was not in his nature to live. But it is different in war. There was only one possibility, one point of view from which it could be justified: the free willing of it. And that in turn was possible only because there was the conviction that Germany was in the right and had the duty to defend herself. At the beginning it would have been wholly impossible for me to conceive of letting the boys go as parents *must* let their boys go now, without inwardly affirming it—letting them go simply to the slaughterhouse. That is what changes everything. The feeling that we were betrayed then, at the beginning. And perhaps Peter would still be living had it not been for this terrible betrayal. Peter and millions, many millions of other boys. All betrayed.

That is why I cannot be calm. Within me all is upheaval, turmoil.[61]

Then, unexpectedly, Germany's western front collapsed: the Fatherland was being defeated. New troops of German youth were ordered to come forth; and in response to this fresh draft, Käthe wrote a short protest article. *Vorwärts*, the SPD newspaper, and the *Vossiche Zeitung*, a socialist daily, printed it in the last week of October 1918.

In the *Vorwaerts* of October 22 Richard Dehmel [a widely read poet of her generation] published a manifesto entitled *Sole Salvation*. He appeals to all fit men to volunteer. If the highest defense authorities issued a call, he thinks, after the elimination of the "poltroons" a small and therefore more select band of men ready for death would volunteer, and this band could save Germany's honor.

I herewith wish to take issue with Richard Dehmel's statement. I agree with his assumption that such an appeal to honor would probably rally together a select band. And once more, as in the fall of 1914, it would consist mainly of Germany's youth—what

*150*

is left of them. The result would most probably be that these young men who are ready for sacrifice would in fact be sacrificed. We have had four years of daily bloodletting—all that is needed is for one more group to offer itself up, and Germany will be bled to death. All the country would have left would be, by Dehmel's own admission, men who are no longer the flower of Germany. For the best men would lie dead on the battlefields. In my opinion such a loss would be worse and more irreplaceable for Germany than the loss of whole provinces.

We have learned many new things in these four years. It seems to me that we have also learned something about the concept of honor. We did not feel that Russia had lost her honor when she agreed to the incredibly harsh peace of Brest-Litovsk. She did so out of a sense of obligation to save what strength she had left for internal reconstruction. Neither does Germany need to feel dishonored if the Entente refuses a just peace and she must consent to an imposed and unjust peace. Then Germany must be proudly and calmly conscious that in so consenting she no more loses her honor than an individual man loses his because he submits to superior force. Germany must make it a point of honor to profit by her hard destiny, to derive inner strength from her defeat, and to face resolutely the tremendous labors that lie before her.

I respect the act of Richard Dehmel in once more volunteering for the front, just as I respect his having volunteered in the fall of 1914. But it must not be forgotten that Dehmel has already lived the best part of his life. What he had to give—things of great beauty and worth—he has given. A world war did not drain his blood when he was twenty.

But what about the countless thousands who also had much to give—other things beside their bare young lives? That these young men whose lives were just beginning should be thrown into the war to die by legions—can this really be justified?

There has been enough of dying! Let not another man fall! Against Richard Dehmel I ask that the

words of an even greater poet be remembered:
"Seed for the planting must not be ground."[62]

As this article took the printer's ink, workers, too, were registering their protests to another military draft, by striking in munition factories throughout Germany. These strikes were also protests against the unyielding imperialism with which the government had treated Russia at the negotiations of Brest-Litovsk, when Russia left the war because of internal revolution. In Russia, the Czar had been overthrown, and the Bolshevik Party was leading Russia toward socialism. Inspired by the Bolsheviks, workers became restless under Germany's imperialism, capitalism, and monarchy. More and more workers struck, as they realized that a victory for Germany would mean continuing economic, social, and political impoverishment—for them, as well as for workers in enemy lands.

Few answered the call for the last offensive: Germany was crumbling. The grasp of Prussian militarism and its caste of ruling industrialists was considerably weakened. For the first time since 1848, Germany could found a new government based on its old yearnings for popular democracy and the unity of most of the German-speaking peoples.

As the armistice was signed, sailors mutinied in Kiel. This lit the torch of revolution; within the week, soldiers and workers struck, mutinied, and rebelled throughout Germany. On tanks and decks, in buildings, barracks, fields, and mines, workers and soldiers—influenced by the Russian organization of soviets—spontaneously formed councils. Workers' Councils took effective control over workshops; Soldiers' Councils, over platoons, subverting the military hierarchy.

A renewed hope filled the people.

Soldiers and workers demanded that their authority be recognized, and the monarchy abdicated its power to the Social Democratic Party, which established a temporary six-member council. The spirit of socialism swept Germany as hundreds of thousands of workers struck day after day to form Councils, to shift the economic power from the hands of their bosses—and their bosses' bosses—into their own.

Käthe participated in this exciting, optimistic upheaval, attending meetings of the Workers' and Artists' Councils.

Though she rarely spoke, she listened intently to the round of discussion on artists as workers in the revolution.

*Revolution 1918*, a charcoal drawing, transmits the passion, chaos, and joy of the working classes as they scream, wave, and reach out to each other in the heat of revolution. Sailors and civilians stand in unity at the Brandenburg Gate, one of the ancient "gates of the city." Though it appears that Kollwitz drew *Revolution 1918* hastily, with dark, short strokes, the work's historical authenticity and immediacy have given it a lasting power.

Near Christmas 1918, Käthe and Hans attended a revolutionary Freedom Celebration.

> I came too late, but in time to hear Breitscheid (harsh, twangy, imperious voice) and two movements of the Ninth Symphony with Strauss conducting. Divinely beautiful. The first time the Ninth has been played since the beginning of the war. And again I was carried away, swept up out of the partisan dust to heights of purest joy. Yes, in the Ninth there is socialism in its purest form. That is humanity, glowing darkly like a rose, its deepest chalice drenched with sunlight.[63]

The dreams of Kollwitz and of many socialists, however, were not matched by the actions of the temporary SPD government leadership. That December, at their first congress, the Workers' and Soldiers' Councils formulated demands that included the further socialization of key industries and a purge of the army, to be replaced by a people's militia. Germany's quartermaster, in titular command of the army, informed the SPD that if the party accepted these demands, he would resign. The temporary leaders—though elected by the workers and soldiers—yielded to the army commander's position; unlike their revolutionary constituents, the leaders were conservative constitutionalists who feared a Russian-like state of turmoil within Germany. The SPD met none of the revolution's major demands—democratization of the army, public control of heavy industry, and redistribution of land and property. Instead, the SPD government decided that its next step would be to hold national elections in a month—on January 9, 1919.

Predictably, this stalemate precipitated a counterwave of further radicalization of workers and soldiers. Hoping to channel the restlessness of the workers into revolutionary actions which would continue the struggle, Rosa Luxemburg and Karl Liebknecht now formed the German Communist Party. Liebknecht was a former leader of the SPD; Luxemburg, a major economic theorist, had organized the extreme left wing of the SPD, which split off to become the Spartacus League upon the SPD's joining the government at the outbreak of the war.

Kollwitz was favorable to the Communists, and would have supported them if they had not advocated violence. She wanted a democratic Germany but not violent civil revolution. She could endure no more bloodshed. Peter's death and her subsequent emotional and intellectual struggle had transformed her into an immovable pacifist. She opposed any group that encouraged further bloodshed as a solution to Germany's problems. With great misgivings she voted, for the first time in a national election, for the reinstatement of the SPD.

A few days later, Liebknecht and Luxemburg were arrested and assassinated by their guards, members of the counterrevolutionary *Freikorps* ("Free Corps"). Kollwitz used the adjectives "despicable" and "infuriating" to describe the murders.

Rosa Luxemburg's body had been heaved into a canal; but Karl Liebknecht's corpse lay in state. On the morning of the funeral, Kollwitz visited the Liebknecht home to offer sympathy to the family. At their request, she made additional drawings of the martyred leader. She thought Liebknecht looked "very proud."[64] There were red flowers around his forehead, where he had been shot.

The deaths of Liebknecht and Luxemburg quelled Germany's hopes for an economic, political, and social revolution. Kollwitz began to plan a memorial piece, using her Liebknecht sketches. She no longer had the patience or the eye to etch, so she decided to try lithography instead.

> I am trying the Liebknecht drawing as a lithograph. ... Lithography now seems to be the only technique I can still manage. It's hardly a technique at all, it's so simple. In it only the essentials count.[65]

With the advent of the ostensibly more liberal Weimar Republic in 1919, Kollwitz became the first woman elected to full professorship at the Prussian Academy of Arts. She was "opposed to all titles,"[66] and refused to use this one, but she accepted the position, and with it, a large, fully equipped studio with side rooms. As a result of the organizing done by the Women's Organization of the SPD and the bourgeois women's movement, women had demanded and received suffrage at the very beginning of the Weimar Republic. A Women's Bureau was set up as part of the National Ministry of Interior, and a respected feminist from the bourgeois women's movement, Gertrud Bäumer, was selected as its administrator.

In her new Academy studio, Kollwitz drew a picture of huddling, protective mothers, and decided to try this theme, with variations, as a lithograph. In *Die Mütter* [Mothers], Kollwitz combined her five major themes—herself; the relationship of a mother to her children; the life of the proletariat (exemplified in women); death as a force (rather than as an evil); and war—in one pure and powerful statement. Kollwitz showed mothers hearing the death knell of poverty and war threatening their children.

In *Mothers* four women crowd close to one another; one, in the left corner, cups her "Kollwitz" hands over her eyes as she weeps, shaking uncontrollably. The lines of her fingers run from her face like wavy rivers of tears. Next to her a poor mother nestles a sleeping tot to her with one hand, while with the other she clutches her young boy. The woman next to her, the most prominent of the group, has the artist's body and face. Two boys look out innocently from the tight enclosure of her arms, which cross each other heavily over the neck of the shorter boy. Her face, closed eyes, and body lean into theirs as if she sought to lose herself in them. (Kollwitz drew a similar pose of herself and one of her sons in 1903, in *Woman with Dead Child*, and again in the 1910 drawing and etching, *Death, Woman, and Child*.) The artist's pose with her children displays more than protective maternal instinct; it shows that the children are her life. The other children in the picture receive their lives from their mothers, but in Kollwitz' case it is she who seeks sustenance from them. The mother next to her, a working-class woman, emits fear and powerlessness as she holds her baby close to her face. *Mothers* is a haunting lithograph of helpless mothers who clutch desperately to life—their children—as they stand close to one another, instinctively trying to protect themselves and each other against the dominant death-dealing forces of poverty and war.

Käthe's own mother now lived with her and Karl, in the top room of their home, the attic room. Katharina was rapidly succumbing to senility, and it saddened Käthe to see this strong, capable woman in a feeble state. Her mother now lived in the world of her children, nieces, and nephews of forty years ago. She had been, Käthe thought, a good mother, although unemotional and even impersonal. It gratified Käthe that her mother's thoughts as an old woman turned again and again to the care, enjoyment, and love of her children. As a daughter, but even more deeply as a mother herself, Käthe felt closer to the older woman than ever before, for the two shared a common love and knowledge—to her mother, as to herself, her children, after all, "were the strongest emotion in her life."[67]

## NOTES

1 Kollwitz, *Diary and Letters*, p. 3.
2 *Ibid.*
3 *Ibid.*, p. 6.
4 *Ibid.*, p. 55.
5 *Ibid.*, p. 54.
6 *Ibid.*, pp. 55–56.
7 *Ibid.*, p. 2.
8 *Ibid.*, p. 7.
9 *Ibid.*, pp. 51–52.
10 *Ibid.*, p. 57.
11 *Ibid.*, p. 53.
12 *Ibid.*, p. 52.
13 *Ibid.*, p. 57.
14 *Ibid.*, p. 43.
15 Heilborn, *Die Zeichner*, p. 10.
16 Bonus-Jeep, *Sechzig Jahre*, p. 107.
17 Kollwitz, *Diary and Letters*, p. 4.
18 Bonus-Jeep, *Sechzig Jahre*, p. 56.
19 Kollwitz, *Diary and Letters*, p. 138.
20 *Ibid.*, p. 59.
21 *Ibid.*, p. 53.
22 Bonus-Jeep, *Sechzig Jahre*, p. 104.
23 *Tagebuchblätter*, 1909–1943, Akademie der Künste Archiv, West Berlin. Entry dated June 1913.
24 *Ibid.*, September 1913.
25 Kollwitz, *Diary and Letters*, p. 53.
26 *Ibid.*, p. 59.

27 Hajo Holborn, *A History of Modern Germany: 1840-1945* (New York: Alfred A. Knopf, Inc., 1969), p. 350.
28 William Harbutt Dawson, *What is Wrong with Germany?* (London: Longmans, Green, and Co., 1913), p. 119.
29 Holborn, *A History*, p. 426.
30 Dawson, *What is Wrong*, p. 110.
31 Kollwitz, *Diary and Letters*, pp. 141-42.
32 *Ibid.*, p. 93.
33 *Ibid.*, p. 62.
34 *Ibid.*, p. 7.
35 *Ibid.*, p. 62.
36 *Ibid.*, p. 8.
37 *Ibid.*, pp. 7-8.
38 *Ibid.*, p. 63.
39 *Tagebuchblätter*. Entry dated New Year's Day, 1914.
40 Kollwitz, *Diary and Letters*, p. 8.
41 *Ibid.*, p. 64.
42 *Ibid.*, p. 143.
43 *Ibid.*, p. 63.
44 *Ibid.*, p. 72.
45 *Ibid.*, p. 70.
46 *Ibid.*, p. 67.
47 *Ibid.*, p. 65.
48 *Ibid.*, pp. 70-71.
49 *Ibid.*, p. 69.
50 *Ibid.*
51 Letter from Selma Waldman to Sue Davidson, dated September 23, 1975.
52 Kollwitz, *Diary and Letters*, pp. 68-69.
53 *Ibid.*, p. 67.
54 *Ibid.*, p. 155.
55 Willy Kurth, *Kunstchronik*, n.f., vol. XXXVII (Berlin, 1916/17), pp. 309-311.
56 Kollwitz, *Diary and Letters*, p. 81.
57 *Ibid.*, p. 157.
58 *Ibid.*, p. 82.
59 *Ibid.*, p. 83.
60 *Ibid.*, p. 94.
61 *Ibid.*, pp. 87-88.
62 *Ibid.*, pp. 88-89.
63 *Ibid.*, pp. 89-90.
64 Bonus-Jeep, *Sechzig-Jahre*, p. 163.
65 Kollwitz, *Diary and Letters*, p. 94.
66 *Ibid.*, p. 160.
67 *Ibid.*, p. 95.

# 7

# I wish
# I might go on working for
# many long years.

*Sunshine streamed* through the skylight
upon Kollwitz as she reached into a garbage can, grabbed a
handful of clay, broke it into smaller pieces, and slowly, carefully, built up the figure of the mother. As she molded, deep
in concentration, the erect form began to bend under her
hands.

The upright figure was moving forward and down. The
head was making a very slow but perceptible nod, as if the
mother were listening—and agreeing—to the movement. The
arms, cradling the child, were being pushed into free space.
Then, abruptly, the square base of the lower torso resisted,
stopping the thrust; the sculpture held, arched over and down
to a spirit of its own. Now the mother bowed far forward,
holding out her child.[1]

Kollwitz followed the change in the form and lines of the
raw shape, filling in its many holes, rebuilding its areas of
balance and weight. Then, after carefully sponging and covering
the new sculpture, she left the studio.

She went to the Secession show with an Academy colleague. At the exhibition, she "saw something that knocked
me over: [Ernst] Barlach's woodcuts,"[2] the earthy, decorative,
but deceptively simple *Group in a Storm* and *The Good
Samaritan*. In his woodcuts Barlach had captured the lively
directness of the Gothic woodcuts that had inspired him, and

Kollwitz wanted to emulate his work in her own style. Barlach was also a sculptor, and Kollwitz admired his ability to succeed in a new medium. Should she, too, try the new, Gothic-influenced, popular art of woodcuts? She mused in her diary:

> I can no longer etch; I'm through with that for good. And in lithography there are the inadequacies of the transfer paper. Nowadays lithographic stones can only be got to the studio by begging and pleading, and cost a lot of money, and even on stones I don't manage to make it come out right. But why can't I do it any more? The prerequisites for artistic works have been there—for example in the war series. First of all the strong feeling— these things come from the heart—and secondly they rest on the basis of my previous works, that is, upon a fairly good foundation of technique.
>
> And yet the prints lack real quality. What is the reason? Ought I do as Barlach has done and make a fresh start with woodcuts? When I considered that up to now, I always told myself that lithography was the right method for me for clear and apparent reasons.
>
> In woodcuts I would not want to go along with the present fashion of spotty effect. Expression is all that I want, and therefore I told myself that the simple line of the lithograph was best suited to my purposes. But the results of my work, except for the print *Mothers*, never have satisfied me.
>
> For years I have been tormenting myself. Not to speak of sculpture.
>
> I first began the war series as etchings. Came to nothing. Dropped everything. Then I tried it with transfers. There too the results were almost never satisfying.
>
> Will woodcutting do it? If that too fails, then I have the proof that the fault lies only within myself. Then I am just no longer able to do it. In all the years of torment these small oases of joys and successes.[3]

She was her own most severe critic. Perfectionism and great respect for technique can often block an artist's creativity, but her obstinate will eventually overcame her dominant critical attitude.

Her development of the Liebknecht Memorial illustrates her method of graphic work, in which an idea she "saw" developed into a print. The procedure began with drawing; for the Liebknecht Memorial, she drew six quick outline sketches in which she sought the essence of Liebknecht's features and position. In the next stage she drew composition studies; for the Liebknecht she used greasy black crayon, ink, watercolor, and wash to design nine compositions. In the third and final stage she drew specific studies of composition and detail, often details of hands, heads, and attitudinal poses of the body. For the Memorial she made nine variant studies, six of which are body poses of workers; the rest are close-up details of the right hand. After twenty-four drawings she drew the composition, now ready to be printed as a graphic.

The resulting pulls from copper and stone dissatisfied her, however, and she destroyed them. For the past two years she had not found the means of expression for the Liebknecht Memorial. Like every artist, she knew that each subject for artistic expression has its corresponding medium. In a last effort, she tried it as a woodcut, hoping that the new medium would successfully mirror "the powerful impression which the sorrow of hundreds of thousands of people at his grave made."[4]

In *Die Lebenden den Toten. Erinnerung an den 15. Januar 1919* [The Living to the Dead. In Memory of January 15, 1919] she included a rare decorative element: the title and dedication became the bottom frame—also the side—of Liebknecht's coffin, in the manner in which a medieval artisan or a tribal artist would include a notation of the event or subject as part of the work's design. Kollwitz had grown up appreciating household items for their beauty as well as for their use, for the art of decorative woodcutting and woodcarving was popular among the many Slavs and Poles of eastern Germany. This aesthetic link with her childhood undoubtedly helped Kollwitz to control the medium from the first. As an artist, she also inherited the tradition of the old Germanic woodblock in which Dürer had worked and which, in her immediate artistic environment, had influenced such contemporaries as Ernst Ludwig Kirchner, Karl Schmidt-Rottluff, Max Pechstein, and other members of *Die Brücke.*

The words in the cut make the Liebknecht print an elegy of the people. Fourteen adults (including two women, one carrying a child) line Liebknecht's bier in meek, desperate mourning. Though the print is a memorial to the man lying in state in the foreground, grieving workers dominate the scene. One stoops low over Liebknecht, his large-knuckled, muscled hand resting tenderly on the coffin; behind him two workers and a mother and a child repeat the bent arch of his back and of those passing the bier until, at the end of the line, at extreme left, a worker stands nearly upright. Nine workers crowd the background, some stretching for a last look at their beloved leader, while others, in shock, stare into space, or cover tears with their hands. Liebknecht's face is highly stylized: the eyebrows, nose, upper lip and chin jut out in stark profile.

Kollwitz' first woodcut was a powerful memorial to Liebknecht's leadership, as well as to the people's resilient strength. Although, like Liebknecht, the people have been victims of cruel deceit by their economic and political rulers, they have kept their human worth and dignity; their spirit endures. Kollwitz' feeling for her subject was deepened by her personal acquaintance with the Liebknecht family, after Liebknecht's death. Together with others, she had concerned herself with the welfare of the Liebknecht children, whose one stated wish was "to have nothing more to do with politics."[5]

Some members of Liebknecht's German Communist Party, however, objected to the woodcut because the artist was not a Communist. They argued that as a non-Communist, Kollwitz had no right to carve a memorial to their former leader. Their attacks disturbed her deeply. In her diary she expressed the frustration she felt both as an artist harassed by narrow partisan considerations and as a woman uninvolved in the "politics" of the inner, decision-making party circle.

> ... I simply should have been left alone, in tranquillity. An artist who moreover is a woman cannot be expected to unravel these crazily complicated relationships. As an artist I have the right to extract the emotional content out of everything, to let

162

things work upon me and then give them outward form. And so I also have the right to portray the working class's farewell to Liebknecht, and even dedicate it to the workers, without following Liebknecht politically. Or isn't that so?[6]

Despite this attack, Kollwitz remained an independent socialist. She did not retract her broad political position or her memorial. She offered the memorial to be used in a benefit for *Arbeiter-Kunstausstellung* ("Workers' Art Exhibition"). This show, held in a large meeting hall on Petersburgerstrasse, in a workers' neighborhood like her own, sold several hundred prints of the woodcut at a few marks each.[7] (No one paid more than a dollar.) From this substantial income a fund was established for workers and artists in need.

Kollwitz wanted to relieve the countless victims of postwar hunger, unemployment, and poverty by making posters drawing attention to their plight. In *Der Arbeitslose* [Unemployed] a large-boned man idly clasps his hands. Large shirt folds covering his powerful physique heighten the contradiction that this able man is out of work. *Unemployed* pleads for unity among workers for an eight-hour day. In fear of losing their jobs, thousands of workers were putting in ten to twelve hours a day, while others worked eight.

In 1920 she also illustrated leaflets exposing starvation. A familiar scene to her, *Beim Arzt* [At the Doctor's] shows a doctor listening to the heart of a very thin boy. The boy's mother, listless, head in hand, sits by the door. Another handout, *Die Kranke und ihre Kinder* [The Sick Woman and her Children], shows an emaciated woman lying in bed as her three wan young children look meekly at her. The longhand text reads:

> Malnutrition has made this woman very sick. She could be cured with proper care. The food to save her life is available in this country, but she cannot afford the exorbitant prices asked for it. What will become of her children? Every day profiteers are sapping the strength of countless people and preparing them for a premature grave.

In the chaos following the abortive revolution, profiteers had sprung up in many businesses, exploiting urgent needs for food, housing, money, and clothing. These two circulars, part of a series of three, were designed to alert the populace to the message written in capital letters at the bottom of each: "Every Profiteer Should Be Denounced and Reported to the Police!"

Postwar disease and famine had also ravaged Austria. A large-scale aid organization in Vienna asked Kollwitz to do a poster as soon as possible, and she readily agreed. The poster showed Death swinging the lash of famine, as "people—men, women, and children, bowed low, screaming and groaning, file past him."[8] As she welcomed this task, Käthe also despaired of it, for how could a poster possibly heal the people's wounds from war, disease, and famine? Yet she felt that it was her responsibility to respond to this or to any other call for help. Always aware that art has social consequences—consequences that she perceived as ultimately moral—she also realized that it was impossible to gauge the influence of artistic work that sought, in her words, "to arouse and awaken mankind."[9] One morning as she worked on the Viennese lithograph, this conflict erupted within her.

> While I drew, and wept along with the terrified children I was drawing, I really felt the burden I am bearing. I felt that I have no right to withdraw from the responsibility of being an advocate. It is my duty to voice the sufferings of men, the never-ending sufferings heaped mountain-high. This is my task, but it is not an easy one to fulfil. Work is supposed to relieve you. But is it any relief when in spite of my poster people in Vienna die of hunger every day? And when I know that? Did I feel relieved when I made the prints on war and knew that the war would go on raging? Certainly not.[10]

A self-portrait, *Nachdenkende Frau* [Woman Lost in Thought] reflects the artist's introverted mood of 1920: "I am disillusioned with all the hate that is in the world," she wrote, and "I long for Socialism which allows people to live— the world has seen enough murder, lies, and corruption."[11] In the lithograph *Woman Lost in Thought*, the artist's eyes are closed; she does not want to see. Within that year she made three other self-portraits called *Woman Lost in Thought*; and these (two of which are drawings) portray an anguished, fearful, pain-racked Kollwitz. In contrast to these two, the lithograph shows a woman who is valiantly trying to control suffering, rather than be overcome by it. Stylistically, *Woman Lost in Thought* resembles her 1893 self-portrait with Karl, *Young Couple*; these are the only two in which the position of the figure expresses the adamant tone of the picture as much as does the pose of the face and hands. Physically, the pose is also similar to that of Rodin's famous sculpture *The Thinker*. Psychically, however, the two "thinkers" are worlds apart: the man looks down, contemplating the affairs of the world, but the woman, Kollwitz, looks within.

What Käthe saw within, in the spring of 1921, was still not reassuring.

> Low. Low. Touching bottom.
>
> I hope to get through it anyhow. Finish the woodcuts by the time of the Jury. Then the Jury; then a week's rest in Neuruppin, and then it may go better. But no. Poor work right along recently and no longer able to see things right. Then I was ripe for illness and fell ill, and at the same time everything slid and dropped and collapsed with a thoroughness I have not experienced for a long time. Now my work disgusts me so that I cannot look at it. At the same time total failure as a human being. I no longer love Karl, nor Mother, scarcely even the children. I am stupid and without any thoughts. I see only unpleasant things. The spring days pass and I do not respond. A weariness in my whole body, a churlishness that paralyzes all the others. You don't notice how bad you get when in such a state until you are beginning to rise out of it. One horrid symptom is this: not only do you not think a single matter through to the end, but you don't even feel a feeling to the end. As soon as one arises, it is as though you threw a handful of ashes on it and it promptly goes out. Feelings which once touched you closely seem to be behind thick, opaque window panes; the weary soul does not even try to feel because feeling is too strenuous. So that there is *nothingness* in me, neither thoughts nor feelings,

> no challenge to action, no participation. Karl feels
> that I am strange—and nothing matters at all to
> me.[12]

She was living by habit. No joy, love, or power within or without her could expel this "nothingness" from her. She was working as much as possible—the majority of each day—but making no progress; she was suffering from not being able to create. "How shall I find joy outside of the work? Talking to people means nothing at all. Nothing and no one can help me," she wrote during a similar period.[13] As a girl she had had moods in which she could not bring herself to use words to communicate with others, for hours, even days at a time.[14] Now, as an adult, this condition repeated itself: she did not want to speak.

What was this "nothingness"? Could she control it? In the past she had fought against it, trying to will its departure. Now she knew that it had to be waited out. By this time, too, she had come to understand that as painful as these spells of "nothingness" were, they were also probably as essential to her work as the times of "fullness." She analyzed her creative process in a metaphor of tides rising and falling within her—the "nothingness" a fast, receding tide, draining her life-forces, while the "fullness," or oncoming tide, gathered strength slowly and painfully, at last surging forth in powerful waves of its own making. On August 23, 1921, four months after she had recorded her state of "nothingness," she wrote Hans the following:

> ... Today I received a card from the Wentschers,
> from Greece. Frau Wentscher is simply in ecstasy.
> I wonder whether Father and I will ever get to take
> such a voyage. You know I don't really believe it,
> nor do I long for it as intensely as I once did. My
> desire for external experiences has greatly diminished
> of late. It used to be that I thought such experiences
> might help my work. Now that is no longer the case.
> Whether and how I am able to work is altogether
> independent of this kind of experience. The readiness forms in waves inside myself; I need only be on
> the alert for when the tide at last begins to rise
> again.[15]

In 1921 Kollwitz produced an exquisite woodcut of an old woman, *Tod mit Frau im Schoss* [Death with Woman in Lap], in which a tired woman is cradled in the lap and arms of Death—who, in this work, is a thoughtful, appealing, and protective old woman. For the first time in her work, Death's advent or presence appears as no horror of hell, but as a calm, natural place of rest, a safe and welcome companion. The symbols of this austere cut are both literal and academic. A pair of clogs—workers' shoes—lie empty at Death's feet, representing rest after work. In the center foreground a crown of barbed wire lies, symbolizing departure from the rack of life.

> I am no longer expanding outward; I am contracting into myself. I mean that I am noticeably growing old. Alas, alas, I notice it in everything—but worst of all I notice it in my work. Complaining does not help, praying does not help either—*it is so.*[16]

Peter's death, her inevitable aging, and the war had changed her forever. In contrast to the vital, revolutionary Black Anna, with whom she had once identified, the self-portraits done fifteen years later register a major psychological shift. The fiery Black Anna stretches from toes to fingertips in a passionate image of revolt; but in these last four works Kollwitz is fatigued, passive, and introspective. There had been a significant shift in her political perspective, as well.

> In the meantime I have been through a revolution, and I am convinced that I am no revolutionist. My childhood dream of dying on the barricades will hardly be fulfilled, because I should hardly mount a barricade now that I know what they are like in reality. And so I know now what an illusion I lived in for so many years. I thought I was a revolutionary and was only an evolutionary. Yes, sometimes I do not know whether I am a socialist at all, whether I am not rather a democrat instead. How good it is when reality tests you to the guts and pins you relentlessly to the very position you always thought, so long as you clung to your illusion, was unspeakably wrong. I think something of the sort has happened to Konrad. Yes, he—and I too—would

*167*

probably have been capable of acting in a revolutionary manner if the real revolution had had the aspect we expected. But since its reality was highly un-ideal and full of earthly dross—as probably every revolution must be—we have had enough of it. But when an artist like Hauptmann comes along and shows us revolution transfigured by art, we again feel ourselves revolutionaries, again fall for the old deception.[17]

Her politics had matured into a persistent faith in eventual change rather than in the specific, too-often violent programs of ideology. Her fervent love of justice remained, as did her commitment to total political, social, and economic change; but because of Peter's death, she had abandoned support of violence as a means to those ends. His death had led her to the renunciation of all war—including violent revolution. Politically, Kollwitz could be termed an independent socialist, for though she gave her artistic and emotional support to Communists in Russia and Germany, she never joined their ranks as a *political* advocate.

Since 1917 Kollwitz had tried to let her grief and horror of the war surface in a series of prints. She had begun the sequence on copper, but had found the medium inadequate to express the fullness of her feelings as a mother and wife. A few attempts at lithographing *Krieg* [War] also resulted in a pale reflection of her intense emotions. Encouraged by her success with the Liebknecht woodcut, she decided to try to execute *War* as a series of woodcuts.

Plans for woodcuts which are going along with the series on war. Reworked the Vienna poster of Death reaching into the band of children. The more I work, the more there dawns upon me how much there is still to be done. It is like a photographic plate which lies in the developer; the picture gradually becomes recognizable and emerges more and more from the mist. So these days I no longer think that I shall soon be able to return to sculpture. Since I have been doing woodcuts I find the technique full of temptations. But above all I am afraid of sculpture. I suppose it is an insuperable problem for me; I am too old ever really to conquer it. It is

*168*

not impossible that I shall gradually move from woodcut technique to woodcarving. But that is still very nebulous.[18]

She wanted to use an almost grainless wood so that she could print as many portfolios of the cycle as possible. She chose pear tree wood, which has a very fine grain, in which to carve her gut responses to the war.[19] Kollwitz' technical expertise, with the very blackest of ink and the natural directness of the medium, gave all seven of the woodcuts in *War* a stark and immediate quality.

Historic incidents had provided the inspiration for her two earlier cycles, *The Revolt of the Weavers* and *The Peasant War*, but *War* was wrested from Kollwitz' own life. An impassioned protest against the gross senselessness of war, the series clearly represents a woman's outrage; it denies men—in any walk of life, but especially in the military—any support whatsoever in waging and perpetuating war. It is one of the twentieth century's superlative graphic statements on the subject.

In the first print, *Das Opfer* [The Victim], a young, nude mother holds out her infant, who lies asleep in the solid, stiff, outstretched cradle of her arms. The mother's eyes are closed, but not in sleep; like her baby, she is an unwilling victim as she offers the life she has borne. In the artist's idiom, "She gives up her child reluctantly; her feet drag."[20] A black semicircle, framed by an arc of white, shows the symbolic darkness and wholeness of the womb; the heads of the baby and the mother protrude slightly from this circle, suggesting that they are in an unnatural position outside it.

*Die Freiwilligen* [The Volunteers] captures the highest, most incredible peak of war hysteria. The skeleton of Death, at extreme left, bangs a loud, relentless beat on a toy circus drum as five young men, screaming in patriotic frenzy, are pulled toward Death by the thunderous, dangerous drumbeat. The great swings of the drummer's hands—one stretched high above Death's head as the other rebounds from the beat—create an image of a powerful, unstoppable, and cruel cadence. *The Volunteers* is a grotesque caricature of men who fall into the march of war; all are misshapen as they reel to Death's downbeat. One eye of the central, most prominent volunteer looks away from Death, while his other eye is shut, giving him an eerie aura of mindlessness. Death's eyes are two gutted pits: his chin is roughly cross-hatched; he shows no emotion, only mechanical duty. This woodcut deserves to be ranked with Picasso's *Guernica* as one of our century's two greatest works of antiwar art.

The next print, *Die Eltern* [The Parents], had begun years earlier as a quick offhand sketch. On November 6, 1917, Kollwitz noted:

> A very good day for me, although it began miserably. I went to the Barlach show, which is very fine. While I was looking at it I was overcome by the restless feeling that I must go to the studio and get to work. Worked tranquilly and well on the relief. Then hit upon a new idea as a result of working. Or rather the same motif, but sculptured in the round. Made a quick sketch, the man and woman kneeling in front, leaning against one another. Her head very low on his shoulder. Her left arm dangles over his right shoulder. Her right arm hangs hopelessly, touching his. His head rests on her back. He is holding his hand over his eyes.[21]

The composition of *The Parents* had caught her imagination: she was on active, intense search for its form, as if she were listening—very hard—to a sweet, faint music, hoping that it would become louder.

> I worked on the sketch again today. I can carry it out only if I really succeed in finding a form that is adequate to the content. It must not be realistic, and yet it cannot be anything but the human form we know. Inventing a form as Krauskopf does is impossible for me; I am no expressionist in that sense. So there remains for me only the familiar human form, but it must be thoroughly distilled.[22]

She knew she needed a new form for *The Parents* but had no idea what that new form would be.

> I have the hope that this time something really new in drawing and etching will come into the work. It can only happen through greater simplicity. Just as I want to make these parents—simplicity in feeling, but expressing the *totality of grief.*[23]

*170*

By 1922 the search had ended. The medium of woodcut supplied the form: *The Parents*, as Kollwitz had originally conceived them, took their place as the third print in the series on war.

In the fourth print, *Die Witwe I* [The Widow I], a young proletarian woman stands pregnant before us, her head hanging low in a pose of woe. Her large hands rest tenderly over her breasts and abdomen. By this time, Kollwitz' creation of large-knuckled, muscled hands had become so dominant in her work that the image had become known as the "Kollwitz hand." In *The Widow I* the "Kollwitz hands" rest protectively over the woman's stomach, at once feeling and protecting the life of the newborn.

In the next plate, *Die Witwe II* [The Widow II], a young working-class woman lies prostrate, her infant dead upon her breast.

The artist described the sixth print as "mothers standing in a circle, defending their children, as sculpture in the round."[24] *Die Mütter* [The Mothers] shows women and children huddled together. The women hold each other and their children in strong, shielding embraces. They look out with fearful but determined eyes; one holds up her hands, palms pushing out, as if to say: "Don't dare come near." The simple sculptural cluster of *The Mothers* is one of the most eloquent visual feminist statements to be found in Western art.

The final print also embodies a feminist response to war, for the hope of *Das Volk* [The People] is a woman. This frame shows the pained, distorted faces of five men—and the composed, enduring countenance of one woman. The woman stands in the center of the men, her "Kollwitz hand" covering a tiny child. Abstracted, and as mysterious as a madonna's, her face mirrors wisdom and strength through love.

In 1923, while completing her years of work on *War*, Kollwitz explained to a colleague, Erna Krüger, that this work represented an attempt to come to terms with the years 1914–1918.

> Everything has gone so well with me concerning my work. I am very busy with the woodcut series on the war. Completely occupied. If there is a section I have not re-worked, I do not know about it. On this

note a work of many years is finally coming to a close. No one would guess that these seven woodcuts of medium size encompass a work of many years, and yet, it is so. They include an analysis of the piece of life that the years of life 1914–1918 encompass. These four years were very difficult to grasp. The large sculpture work that I wanted to make for the fallen volunteers [Peter's Memorial] I don't really expect to accomplish any more. So this series of woodcuts is a more humble attempt to grasp and express that time. In the near future I only have smaller works in mind. I have received a commission from the International Trade Union Congress to make a poster against war. That is a task that makes me happy. Some may say a thousand times, that this is not pure art, which has a purpose. But as long as I can work, I want to be effective with my art.[25]

When the *War* woodcuts were printed as a portfolio in 1923, postwar inflation had reached its peak and banks were collapsing daily. In that year the bottom dropped out of the value of the Deutsche Mark. The printing presses could not keep up with the inflation. Baskets and eventually wheelbarrows were needed to carry the worthless money from the pay counter and then as quickly as possible to the grocery store before the mark dropped further in value. Widespread hunger caused disease, death, and destitution among thousands of poor and middle-class Germans. The line of working-class women, men, and children waiting to see Karl at the free morning clinic stretched from his office down two flights of stairs to the street.

Like thousands of others, Käthe and Karl lost much of their life savings during this period. She described the desperate times to Jeep.

It's very strange here. Margarine costs almost one million marks [$15,000.00] a pound, and you only get that after standing in a long queue for a long time. It's inevitable that it will all come to unrest. One can't buy provisions, and many of the shelves are empty. Every day we give out a half million marks, sometimes even more, for food.

It's easy to become fearful about where all this money is going to come from.[26]

In this year she carved out of the agony of hunger, which was all around her, a small, heart-wrenching woodcut entitled *Hunger* [Starvation]. An old woman, hands holding her head, shrieks like an animal for food. Below her protruding ribs, grotesquely disproportionate breasts droop low, almost to her knees, creating a pathetic figure deformed by lack of food.

With this woodcut, along with the lithograph *Wien Stirbt! Rettet Seine Kinder!* [Vienna is dying! Save her children!] and the antiprofiteering leaflets, Kollwitz confirmed her commitment to the use of her art for the sake of bettering human conditions. During this period she wrote:

> At such moments, when I know I am working with an international society opposed to war, I am filled with a warm sense of contentment. I know, of course, that I do not achieve pure art in the sense of Schmidt-Rottluff's, for example. But still it is art. Everyone works the way he can. I am content that my art should have purposes outside itself. I would like to exert influence in these times when human beings are so perplexed and in need of help. Many people feel the obligation to help and exert influence, but my course is clear and unequivocal. . . .
>
> . . . I wish I might go on working for many long years as I am working now.[27]

The society of which she spoke was undoubtedly The Women's International League for Peace and Freedom, an active women's organization dedicated to peace, disarmament, and international cooperation that had sprung up in 1915. Kollwitz had offered the League some of her work—particularly lithographs of war-stricken mothers and children—to be distributed as postcards.[28]

In 1924, five years after suffrage, the German women's movement was making modest but steady progress against discrimination in labor, politics, education, and the professions. The thirty women representatives who now sat in the Reichstag were responsible for the innovative social legislation that protected expectant mothers against being discharged from their jobs due to pregnancy. Militant feminists brought abortion, prostitution, and the double standard of morality to public attention, challenging laws that discriminated against both married women and unmarried mothers with children. For the abortion campaign Kollwitz contributed her skill as an artist, lithographing the poster *Nieder mit dem Abtreibungsparagraphen!* [Abolish the Abortion Law!]. These words, written in bold longhand, draw attention to a poor working-class woman crowded by three children. The gaunt, very pregnant woman, like her tiny, thin children, wears a hopeless, fearful look; she seems to ask, "Where will we find enough food?"

Kollwitz also lent her support to a movement that had paralleled the women's movement—the homosexual rights movement. Along with more than six thousand others, the majority of whom were professionals, and half of these, doctors, Kollwitz gave her signature to a petition sponsored by the Scientific Humanitarian Committee, calling for the removal of homosexual acts from criminal status, except in cases of force or the involvement of a minor.[29]

Despite such progress, patriarchal practices continued to dominate German life. As one of fifty-nine part-time female professors among some four thousand full-time male professors, Kollwitz enjoyed a relatively privileged position for a woman. In terms of equal opportunities, however, her life, and the life of the average woman, had improved little—if at all—since the 1919 franchise.

Years before, Kollwitz had been intrigued by young Stan and her unconventional feminist attitudes. Now she became interested in another free spirit, "H.W.," an artist who lived contentedly alone. She wondered about "H.W.":

> Perhaps she was among those few women who could really live alone and for themselves. Not without men, but in such a way that men aren't the center of their lives. Most women actually experience their lives through men, or at least they imagine it so. Perhaps H.W. will be able to remain free, an artist who doesn't need anyone but herself, a bohemian in personality.[30]

Käthe acknowledged Stan and "H.W." as kindred spirits, but for her part she had long since answered—if not resolved—the conflict between her professional and personal life by marrying. If she weren't with Karl, she knew she would be living and working in her studio like "H.W.," for no matter how much free time she had been able to spend on her work, she admitted that the responsibilities of marriage had always prevented her from working as much as she wanted to. Still, even in the early, stormy years of marriage, she had relied upon Karl's affection and the security of his love. In her diary she wrote:

> What strength Karl has. At times he is tired, and then he too is unproductive and bored; but then come times when he goes through it like a champion, victorious over his fifty-six years, over all his toilsome labors, over his illness. Then he is wonderful. Shall I have to live without him, or he without me? We will miss one another very much. He inspires, animates me. But best of all is his capacity for love. It comes out of a glad kindness which sometimes seems to me absolutely incredible. This capacity for love results in his being loved in turn by so many, so many people. Above all by women and children.[31]

At times her union of profession and marriage had combined to make a healthy, stable environment in which she created well. At other times the roles were in conflict, and perhaps this was one of the unconscious causes of her uncreative periods. She didn't know. She did know, however, that she accepted this contradiction in her life as a basic, complex emotional truth. She acknowledged that she needed both Karl *and* her work.

The persistent years of struggle that had made her Germany's lone successful woman artist at last brought Kollwitz recognition by masses of women, in the burgeoning wave of feminism. She hired a woman typist to help answer her growing correspondence from admirers, and, remembering her Aunt Yetta, she answered every letter she received. The vitality of the women's movement provided a sympathetic social milieu for her work, helping her to produce more outstanding pieces of art in her fifties than during any other decade of her life. Her accumulated training in four graphic arts and in sculpture, her additional free time, and her increased maturity also contributed to making the 1920s Kollwitz' most richly productive period. With recognition came greater public responsibilities, a fact of life which did not please her.

> But when I compare the present with the past, the present seems to me not so full. At that time I lived deep inside myself; now my life turns outward too much. The brief morning is devoted to work, the afternoon to everything else, household, letters, seeing people, things in general. The days rush on faster and faster; time for introspection grows shorter and shorter. I feel like a person whose breathing is shallow and fast, though he ought to be taking quiet, deep breaths. All that must be changed.[32]

But complain as she might, her sense of duty made it impossible for her to shirk unwelcome responsibilities.

As she had written to the painter Erna Krüger, the International Trade Union Congress in Amsterdam had invited her to do a poster. In 1923 Kollwitz was one of many respected artists the Congress had commissioned for an antiwar series to be distributed throughout Europe. She had wanted to draw a feminist-oriented picture of "mothers pressed together like animals, protecting their brood in a cluster of black,"[33] but the labor congress preferred a depiction of survivors. She responded with *Die Überlebenden* [The Survivors], which showed those uprooted by the war—"the parents, widows, blind people, and all their children with their fearful, questioning, helpless eyes and pale faces."[34]

In 1924 everyone needed food. People begged on streets, knocked on doors, waited for soup and bread in huge municipal shelters. Kollwitz' conscience could not rest. At the request of the International Worker's Relief Organization, she designed *Deutschlands Kinder Hungern!* [Germany's Children are Starving!]. This accusing message flanked a painful picture of hollow-eyed children holding out empty bowls for food.

As in 1920, Kollwitz again joined other artists to support the workers' fight as they struck for an eight-hour day. Along with 250 other professional artists, Kollwitz offered some of her best work to be sold at an exhibit at the Wertheim Stores in Alexander Platz, central Berlin. After the show had opened, some members of the Help by the Artists group—among them, Georg Grosz, Heinrich Zille and Otto Nagel—undertook, as an additional fund-raising project to benefit the strikers and other economic victims, a special portfolio of lithographs on the subject of hunger.

With only a few days of notice, Kollwitz lithographed a poster entitled *Brot!* [Bread!] for this portfolio. In creating *Bread!* she was in such a hurry that when she discovered she had no transfer paper for her first print, she used the backside of a poster for one of Hauptmann's recent plays. Thus in the first take of *Bread!*, square lines of the busy, loud-colored Hauptmann poster[35] are caught within the flowing lines of the long gray dress of the mother, whose hungry children clamor and tug at her. One screaming child pulls desperately at her dress as the stooped mother, back to us, tries to cover its mouth. In *Bread!* Kollwitz utilized her skill as a lithographer, sculptor, and poster-maker to the full: like the clear image, the single word "Bread!"—written emphatically below the mother's skirt—demonstrates the art of poster-making powerfully and succinctly.

In 1924 Kollwitz lithographed another poster, *Nie Wieder Krieg!* [Never Again War!]. In this work her anger over the war dominates her sorrow. A zealous youth summons others to pacifism: his black eyebrows arch, his hair sweeps back dramatically as he stretches his right arm, first two fingers pointing in a visual exclamation point to the clarion call "Never Again War!," writ large on either side of his arm. This herald dramatizes Kollwitz' urging that "the idealism and readiness for sacrifice of young people should not be turned toward war, but toward building a better life and society."[36] She composed this huge poster for the 1924 Central German Youth Day in Leipzig. Sponsored by the organization *Nie Wieder Krieg*, German Youth Day was a celebration of antiwar rallies and speeches, held annually on the anniversary of the start of World War I, the first day of August. Founded in December, 1919, *Nie Wieder Krieg* was organized to introduce youth to the pacifist sentiments of soldiers and workers.

Because of their instant appeal, these three posters—
*Germany's Children Are Starving!*, *Bread!*, and *Never Again War!*—have been reprinted many times since their creation—
often without Kollwitz' broad, familiar signature and some-
times, unfortunately, pleading causes inimical to Kollwitz'
intent.

In this prolific year, 1924, which could very well be
termed her "poster year," Kollwitz also created the lithograph
*Verbrüderung* [Brotherhood], one of the few pictures in
Western art in which men are shown holding each other
warmly. The older man, on the right, looks resolutely into the
other's face, demanding his trust, while the younger dreams, as
if his companion has given him a vision. Both have rugged,
muscular features. The poster implies Kollwitz' politics, based
on a faith that a spirit of trust and cooperation between working men and their nations—internationalism—would someday
"raise humanity higher than humanity has been."[37] *Brotherhood* holds out this abiding hope for humankind.

Perhaps in *Brotherhood* Kollwitz was responding to the
praise her work had just received in Moscow's first exhibit of
German art. She was well represented in the show, and the
revolutionary Communists hailed her as their own. Acknowl-
edging that if she were young she would certainly be a Communist, she responded in kind to their enthusiasm.[38] To Otto
Nagel, who had organized the exhibit, she wrote:

> I am so glad that the Moscow Exhibition has been
> such a success, and that my work is to remain there.
> I should very much like to visit Russia one of these
> days. . . . The people there, how naturally they be-
> have and how cheerful they are. How nice that
> must be.[39]

Some months later she produced another in her long
series of self-portraits. It shows us a pensive, anxious Käthe;
though the steadiness of her gaze reflects the familiar iron will,
the eyes reveal a certain uneasiness, a fearfulness. The frank-
ness of the self-portrait accurately indicates the artist's
honesty. Kollwitz flattered neither herself nor others. At the
same time, she was not given to criticism or condemnation of
others.[40] Her criticism was largely reserved for herself—both
her conduct and her work.

When the American writer Agnes Smedley—another independent socialist and feminist—visited Kollwitz in 1925, she noted that "in speaking with her one always has the impression that truth alone is of value to her."[41] While she was not a sparkling conversationalist, what Kollwitz said carried weight and persuasive power.[42] Above all, Smedley was impressed by the simplicity of Kollwitz' personality and life-style.

> She is now fifty-eight years of age, and remains unimpressed by attentions, medals, books, or professorships. Her ceaseless physical activity would lead one to believe she is no more than forty. Her life is as simple as that of an ordinary working woman, and she still lives in the workers' section of North Berlin. Her gaze is direct and her voice startlingly strong, and she sees far beyond those who bring her superficial, external tributes or who try to use her for their own propaganda purposes. She is a silent person, but when she speaks it is with great directness, without trimmings to suit the prejudices of her hearers. Many people, before meeting her, expect to see a bitter woman. But they see, instead, a kind—very kind—woman to whom love—strong, love, however—is the rule of life.[43]

Kollwitz was also a very private person who hated being in the limelight. On one of Jeep's customary visits during this period, when Käthe had become a public figure, the two women decided to go shopping; and as they went into central Berlin, many passersby recognized Käthe and greeted her. While she appreciated their friendliness, she was nevertheless embarrassed at being recognized by strangers. At one of the shops, Jeep bought Käthe a small housegift that had to be delivered. As the clerk wrote down "Frau Kollwitz, 25 Weissenburgerstrasse, No. 58," Jeep, turning to Käthe, saw her step back into the corner to avoid the clerk's gaze. On the way home Käthe confided that "life is less pleasant since I have become known."[44]

Kollwitz' simplicity sometimes made her uneasy among her own colleagues and acquaintances. At a party for Lily

(*text continued on page 188*)

179

PLATE 21. *Die Freiwilligen* [The Volunteers], 1922–23, woodcut.

PLATE 22. *Das Volk* [The People], 1922–23, woodcut.

PLATE 23. *Selbstbildnis, im Profil, nach links* [Self-portrait, in profile, facing left] , 1924, woodcut.

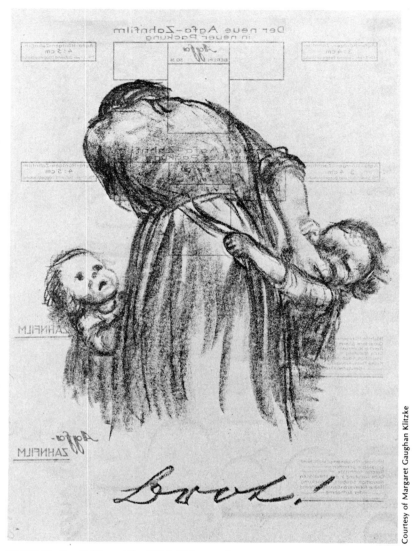

PLATE 24. *Brot!* [Bread!] , 1924, lithograph.

182

PLATE 25. *Kleines Selbstbildnis, nach links* [Small Self-portrait, facing left] , 1924, lithograph.

PLATE 26. *Witwe mit Totem Kind* [Widow with Dead Child], 1923, lithograph.

PLATE 27. Untitled, about 1925, drawing.

PLATE 28. *Mutter, Säugling an ihr Gesicht drückend* [Mother holding her infant close to her face] , 1925, lithograph.

PLATE 29. *Zwei schwatzende Frauen mit zwei Kindern* [Chatting Women], 1930, lithograph.

Braun, whom she had known for many years, she felt uncomfortable because some of the guests, though socialists, were, in appearance and behavior, more like *"grandes dames."* She did not want to dance because she felt as if "someone was observing me with opera glasses."[45]

Within the circle of her family, however, she was more comfortable. The Kollwitz circle now had three generations. Hans had married an artistically talented woman, Ottilie Ehlers, who had borne a son, Peter, and twin daughters, Jordi and Jutta. Käthe's three grandchildren were a source of "great, rich joy."[46]

> The first day of Whitsun, a joyous and happy day for me. I went out to spend it with the children. . . . We sat on the ground in the big, open, polygonal arbor. . . . I am vegetatively happy looking on it all and watching the children crawl all around. Karl and I are the oldest. Then Heinrich and Gertrud, then Hans, Ottilie and Gerda. And then the wild scrambling of the children. And all the colors! Ottilie white, Gerda bright yellow, Hans white linen, Manon pink, Veronika pale orange, little Peter white and particolored with cheeks flushed red with happiness, and the twins in flaming red dresses. The twins are precious. Sturdy, droll, innocent little white heads. Babbling their own language. . . . It is wonderful to see. Happy Ottilie, who is so thoroughly maternal. Whatever comes later on, these three years of work with the babies will always give her a kind of satiated feeling. She is a mother through and through, much as she sometimes rants against being one.
>
> Little Peter has given me a pink.[47]

Kollwitz' capacity for love and tenderness was not confined to the appealing young. The tenderness of her regard for her mother, in the latter's advanced senility, is striking.

> [Mother] likes to have the cat on her lap. . . . It seems more and more evident to me that Mother does not recognize the cat for what it is, but thinks it is a baby. Often she wraps it up in a blanket and holds it just like a child. It is touching and sweet to see my old mother doing this.[48]

In 1925 Kollwitz created a very dark series of woodcuts entitled *Proletariat* [The Proletariat]. The series was executed quickly—in a single year. In this relatively brief period were telescoped the three major stages of her creative process. The inspiration for a new work came as the tide of *nothingness* receded and she became filled with energy. Next came the second stage, "when a real and happy interest exists, and there are no doubts about the work's essential rightness."[49] This was the time she cherished most, working surely day by day, at her creative peak: "How wonderful life is at such times."[50] The last stage followed when the work was under control, well within grasp, but now less a pleasure than a drudgery, for it had to be finished and she felt "driven to complete it."[51]

In *The Proletariat*, as in *War*, the point of view stems from a woman's experience, this time that of a working-class mother. The subject is tragic: death due to poverty.

In the first frame, *Erwerbslos* [Unemployed], a little girl faces us, wide-eyed with terror, clutching an empty spoon. Her tall, gaunt father clutches his neck, as if his hand were a noose. Only half of the mother's face emerges from the black ink, her grim, thin-lipped mouth turned down. The second frame, *Hunger* [Starvation], shows terrified women and children crawling through thick darkness, as Death—a skull—brandishes a lasso over their heads. *Kinder sterben* [The Children Die], the final frame, is the sharpest and most emphatic of the series. Stupefied with grief, a mother holds a child's coffin in her work-muscled hands. Thin, long-knived strokes abstract her features, giving her face the imperishable quality of rock.

With the completion of *The Proletariat*, as her friend and comrade artist Otto Nagel noted, Kollwitz "had achieved in her art the simplicity only a genius can afford."[52] It was a genius backed by formidable years in practice: twenty-eight years at etching and lithography; twenty-two years at sculpture; seven years at woodcutting.

On February 16, 1925, Käthe's mother died. At age eighty-seven, Katharina Schmidt had outlived her husband and her oldest daughter, Julie, who had died in 1917.

The influence of her mother upon Käthe's character and work had been profound. Like her mother—and like herself—

the women Kollwitz portrayed are loving *and* strong. It is the women in her work—most often mothers—who carry the drama. With few exceptions, men participate in Kollwitz' emotional scene as adjuncts, as fathers and husbands in the background. It is the women who confront the crises head on: they brave war, poverty, homelessness, their husband's unemployment, servitude, widowhood, sexual abuse, and their children's hunger. In the darkest despair, the women continue to support the life of others. Kollwitz' women are subjected but not humiliated, victimized by force but not weak; they have the power—through strong love—to face and endure their trials. Her women are heroic in the epic of every day.

Romantic love was not one of Kollwitz' subjects. Only in her *Secreta* drawings—which she never showed to anyone—did she depict erotic, romantic love between woman and man.[53]

For Kollwitz, love and responsibility were linked. Her own capacity for love extended beyond those closest to her to a reverence for all life, and a responsibility to all human beings.

It was a heavy burden, but she faltered under it only during the First World War, when, "half alive and half dead, one crawled in silence."[54] At that time, following Peter's death, she had believed "I would go crazy with grief."[55] Yet she had not only endured but grown.

And the work begun then—the memorial—was not yet finished.

With Karl she now wanted to visit the Belgian cemetery where Peter lay buried. They had never seen Roggevelde, the World War I cemetery, and Käthe also wanted an understanding of the space where the two figures of Peter's memorial would stand. In June, 1926, they traveled to western Belgium.

> The cemetery is close to the highway.... The entrance is nothing but an opening in the hedge that surrounds the entire field. It was blocked by barbed wire which [a friendly young man] bent aside for us; then he left us alone. What an impression: cross upon cross.... on most of the graves there were low, yellow wooden crosses. A small metal plaque in the center gives the name and number. So we

found our grave. . . . We cut three tiny roses from a flowering wild briar and placed them on the ground beside the cross. All that is left of him lies there in a row-grave. None of the mounds are separated; there are only the same little crosses placed quite close together. . . . and almost everywhere is the naked, yellow soil. . . . at least half the graves bear the inscription *allemand inconnu.* [unknown German] . . . .

We considered where my figures might be placed. . . . What we both thought best was to have the figures just across from the entrance, along the hedge. . . . Then the kneeling figures would have the whole cemetery before them. . . . Fortunately no decorative figures have been placed in the cemetery, none at all. The general effect is of simple planes and solitude. . . . Everything is quiet, but the larks sing gladly.

As we went on, we probably passed the very place where he fell, but here everything has been rebuilt. . . . Everywhere there are traces of the war. . . . the ground is hollowed out by countless shellholes. . . . In this place alone the Germans are said to have lost 200,000 men in the course of the four years. Their trenches and the Belgian trenches were sometimes separated by only twenty, even ten yards. They have been closed up now and life goes on; only the Belgian dugouts and trenches, those bowels of death as they call them, have been preserved and are a sort of place of pilgrimage for the Belgians. . . .[56]

That night they stayed in the nearest village, Dixmuide, where, prophetically, she dreamed there would be another war.[57]

After seeing Roggevelde Käthe was highly motivated to work on Peter's Memorial. Now, as she sculpted *Die Mutter* [The Mother] and *Der Vater* [The Father], she could visualize the space in which they would stand. With renewed assurance she wrote to Jeep that she was working diligently now.

You know, then, I am very happy. Every day is then important. The only unsettling thing is that something will call me away from the work before it is ready. At no other time does Death seem so close or unwanted as when I am working on something that is important to me. Then I am very economical with my time. But when I can't work, I am lazy in every way and waste my time. So wish me a long life, so I can finish![58]

In 1926 she joined a group of German and Austrian women artists in founding GEDOK, or *Gesellschaft der Künstlerinnen und Künstfreunde* [Society for Women Artists and Friends of Art].[59] The organization was dedicated to showing, sponsoring, and contributing to the work of women artists. A cultural offshoot of the popular women's movement, GEDOK was clearly feminist in purpose. Like the Secession, the group was organized to bypass the elitist route of the dealer, so that women artists could have direct contact with the public. While the Secession had been formed in opposition to academic prejudice, GEDOK was founded, thirty-three years later, to counteract sex bias.

At about this time—perhaps for GEDOK's first exhibition —Kollwitz made some studies entitled *Frauenasyl* [Shelter for Homeless Women]. These are distressing portraits of anxious children and distraught women crowded into cot-lined rooms.

Nineteen twenty-seven marked Käthe's sixtieth year. Ten years earlier she had recorded a daydream of how she would like to live from her sixtieth year on.

Today, as I returned from going on calls with Karl, the weather had that half springlike quality that always starts me daydreaming—I imagined the following picture of my old age.... At some pretty place nearby—say, Ferch—Karl and I will have a cottage with a garden, a small potato field, at least one dog. We will work in the garden and each of us will go about his own pursuits. Karl will do scientific research and I, as far as I am still able, small sculptures and drawings. Above all we will live in nature and will have with us a few children whom we will take from the city for the whole long summer. City children. They will go to the village school and play about in the open, learn to swim, to row, and so on. If they could be our own grandchildren—how wonderful that would be. But if not, then strangers' children. The plan calls for money, but by then we will have it. Many books! If the winter proves too long, we would go to Berlin for a few months. Faithful old Lina would take care of the household; some nice young girl—we know many of them—would be in charge of the children. Four or five children, I think. That would be a lovely life.[60]

This dream had not come true; she was still on Weissenburger-strasse, but she was not really sad about it. She knew that "for all my romantic feeling for the country, I suppose I need the city,"[61] its stimulating people and activities.

As she had done a decade earlier, Käthe now began to prepare a retrospective show to commemorate her birthday. In February 1927, a Beethoven piano concert moved her to recall an image that had occupied her for a long time: "the woman watching who feels everything,"[62] not a mother, but a woman who "knows about the world's suffering"[63] and who conveys, like some of Beethoven's adagios, pure soul without words.

While it was not Kollwitz' deliberate intention, the retrospective did feature the image of a woman "who feels everything": Kollwitz's self-portraits themselves reveal, year by year, the ineluctable signature of experience on the artist's face. Only the first, as a student, pictures her in laughter.[64] Kollwitz never again chose to portray herself thus. Until 1916 many of the self-portraits seem to ask, "Is this woman's lot, to suffer?" From 1916 on, however, the studies seem to absorb the question and supply the answer—sometimes in fear, sometimes in anger, but with the intelligence, dignity, and courage required to live as a woman in a world of war, poverty, oppression, and their attendant anguish.

Early in 1927, with characteristic modesty, she wrote, "I shall never approach those great ones,"[65] but it was clear, by July, that she had. The 1927 show at Cassirer's was a crowning joy.

To top it off, the Soviet Union now invited Kollwitz and her husband to participate (all expenses paid) in the celebration of its tenth birthday as a Communist society. Käthe had wanted to visit the Soviet Union, at least since 1924, and felt honored at being asked to show her work as part of the commemorative ceremonies. In 1927, in *Arbeiters International Zeitung* ("The Workers' International Paper"), she described her position with regard to Communist Russia.

> This is not the place for us to discuss why I am not a Communist. But it is the place for me to state that, as far as I am concerned, what has happened in Russia during the last ten years seems to be an event which both in stature and significance is comparable only with that of the great French Revolution. An old world, sapped by four years of war and undermined by the work of revolutionaries, fell to pieces in November 1917. The broad outline of a new world was hammered together. In an essay written during the early days of the Soviet Republic, [Maksim] Gorki speaks of "flying with one's soles turned upwards. [*sic*] " I believe that I too can sense such flying in the gale inside Russia. For this flying of theirs, for the fervour of their beliefs, I have often envied the Communists.[66]

The Bolsheviks appreciated art that sought to unify people by portraying common social experience; they held this moral principle of art as essential. Education, also, was based on the ethic of the community rather than that of the individual. Given this viewpoint, it is probably not surprising that the Russians welcomed Kollwitz, in November, as the artistic spirit of the revolution. Muscovites crowded her three-day exhibit, held in an unpretentious suite of high-ceilinged rooms. An interpreter helped her to speak with the people who had made the revolution.

Kollwitz' vision of an egalitarian society seemed to live in the hearts and actions of ordinary Russians. She was especially impressed by the major event of the tenth anniversary—a colorful mass rally in Moscow's main square. At the end of the speeches, mass calisthenics, and dramatics events, everyone crossed arms to sing and sway to the revolutionary "Propeller Song." Käthe was also touched by another, more private scene at the demonstration: a young working-class father and his two children, the daughter in his lap and the son by his side, absorbing a political speech with inspired, believing faces. Both these scenes resulted in lithographs. From the family scene she created, in 1927, a simple portrait entitled *Zuhörende* [Listening]. Later, in 1932, at the request of Russian artists—in order to clarify her position on the "imperialist war against Russia"—she made *Wir schützen die Sowjetunion* (*Das Propellerlied*) [We protect the Soviet Union (The Propeller Song)].[67] Four workers, one of them a woman, demonstrate solidarity as they link hands, singing and swaying.

Käthe and Karl returned from their Russian experience "as if we had both had a good airing."[68] Rejuvenated, Käthe decided to make another image of candid affection, inspired by a biblical painting that had greatly moved her four years previously. It was

> . . . a painting by an unknown of around 1440: the Trinity. To the right you see the meeting of Mary and Elisabeth. They stand facing one another, dressed in wide mantles which enfolded the whole into one group. They are holding their mantles open, and in their swollen abdomens you see the coming children, Jesus and John. The faces are earnest and dedicated.[69]

Feeling the communion between the two expectant mothers, she now transferred onto paper a very tender scene. In her final, 1928, version, Elizabeth, the future mother of John, slightly the elder of the two women, gently touches the round abdomen of Mary and comforts her with a kiss, as if whispering to the younger, "Don't worry, it will be all right." The future mother of Jesus limply hangs her hands, a gesture that conveys uncertainty; her eyes are closed as she bows her head slightly in humility to receive Elizabeth's kiss. Though Kollwitz chose for *Maria und Elisabeth* [Mary and Elizabeth] the medium of woodcut—which is harsher than that of the lithograph—each of her three versions of the scene is pervaded by a warm graciousness. The historical background of *Mary and Elizabeth* is biblical, but the image is maternal and sisterly, a visual poem of caring between women.

In 1928 Kollwitz was promoted to become the first woman department head at the Prussian Academy of Arts. Now she taught the master graphics class, the most advanced level of academic training in the graphic arts. With her formal appointment in May, she became a full-time Prussian civil servant. For the first time in her life, at age sixty-one, she received a regular income—a little more than two hundred dollars a month. The delay in this full recompense was due not to her own indifference (she wanted to relieve Karl of the long working hours their combined needs had required of him) but most likely to the longstanding prejudice against professional women whose husbands were "gainfully employed."

By 1928 four large federations of women's organizations had coalesced, joining millions of women to form Germany's largest, most powerful bloc of voters. The four included the Federation of German Women's Clubs, made up of thirty-six organizations of feminist, vocational, and religious concerns; the League of German University Women, comprising the first professional union of women teachers, doctors, lawyers, professors, and university students; the Federation of German Women's Vocational Organizations, consisting of active union and non-union working women; and the vast union of Protestant Women's Clubs and Catholic Women's Clubs. In the 1928 elections, this coalition helped to rally twenty-nine million voters to the Social Democratic Party, to the numerous middle-class parties, and to the Catholic Center Party. As a result, the National Socialist Workers' (Nazi) Party, with less than a million votes, was soundly defeated.

But not for long.

For the second time since the end of World War I, Germany was plunged into chaos. It was fortunate for Kollwitz that she was now able to supplement the family income, for postwar inflation had added artisans, black-coated workers, and peasants to the long list of destitute Germans that already included bankrupt property owners and merchants. Over three million unemployed stood in orderly bread lines. In October 1929, the Wall Street crash increased that number on the streets of Germany.

The economy, heavily dependent on foreign loans and markets, collapsed.

The economic crisis caused millions of desperate members of the lower middle class—civil servants, teachers, small shopkeepers, pensioners—to turn to the remedies offered by the National Socialist party headed by the fanatical Adolf Hitler. Behind the scenes, the old triumvirate—industrialists, land-owners and bankers—also supported Hitler, in order to further its interests against the labor unions and to profit by the remilitarization of Germany. The racist, antidemocratic dogma of the Nazis appealed both to many members of the lower-middle class and to the privileged classes; and Hitler's aggressive foreign policy stance answered to certain popular national aspirations as well.

In the September 1930 elections, the National Socialists rallied the support of more than six million voters. The urban workers were not won at this time—either by the appeal of the Nazis or by that of the Communists—but continued their support of the Social Democratic Party. In fact, the working-class electorate generally resisted Hitler's demagoguery in this election, giving support either to the SPD or to the Communist Party. The Catholic Center Party also retained firm support in 1930. Nevertheless, Nazi strength in the Reichstag was now second only to that of the Social Democratic Party.

In this position, the National Socialists launched aggressive political attacks against the government. Among these were opposition to the unemployment fund and resistance to SPD attempts to impose direct taxes. Under this pressure, the SPD ministers resigned, insuring the subsequent rise of National Socialism and the end of any hopes of democratic government the weak Weimar Republic may have inspired.

Kollwitz watched these political developments with deep misgivings. The National Socialists' use of brute force to suppress a workers' rally angered her; it also alerted her to the imminent political danger. She reacted against the political repression by drawing *Demonstration*, a scene of a workers' rally in which a group of staunch men, singing, protest civil and economic policies.

During this period, Käthe's private world offered some respite from her growing consciousness of the darkness that was descending upon Germany. Yet anxiety was not absent from her delight in Ottilie, Hans, and her grandchildren.

> My feeling of love for these five is often so strong as to be painful. And of the three children it is always

Peter who is closest to our hearts. I do not know quite why it is that Karl and I often tremble with concern over the boy. His face looked so sweet as he walked holding Karl's hand and listening to stories. The white hair, the red cheeks, the frail little hand laid in ours. The beautiful naked little body.[70]

She also turned, as if for reassurance, to common people enjoying simple pleasures. In *Zwei schwatzende Frauen mit zwei Kindern* [Chatting Women], lithographed in 1930, two working-class women sit together on a bench, probably in Karl's clinic, laughing and sharing stories as they absently fondle their children.

During the following year, Käthe completed *Die Mutter* [The Mother] and *Der Vater* [The Father] for the *Gefallenen-Denkmal* [Memorial to the Fallen]. On April 22, 1931, at the Academy, she unveiled the sculptures. Never had she been so animated, excited, or nervous at one of her openings. She experienced the event as "a great divide, a highly significant period."

> For years I worked on them in utter silence, showed them to no one, scarcely even to Karl and Hans; and now I am opening the doors wide so that as many people as possible may see them. A big step which troubles and excites me; but it has also made me very happy because of the unanimous acclaim of my fellow artists. . . . But now that the works are delivered to the world, I am calmer. In June I will start on the finishing touches. In the fall—Peter—I shall bring it to you.[71]

The pair of figures are a triumph. More than any of her work, these sculptures reveal Kollwitz' essential optimism and her power as an artist. Seventeen years before, in the terrible reality of her life without Peter, she had painfully chosen to survive, to dedicate herself to him through her work. With that decision, she had changed her mourning, passive relationship to Peter—and to the world.

The memorial begun for Peter had grown to encompass all the victims of the war. It had been the most difficult trial of Kollwitz' life. Despite her meager knowledge of sculpture at the outset, despite her almost continual doubt and insecurity over the seventeen years devoted to it, the memorial was accomplished. She had kept her vow to Peter.

And beautifully. The sculptures equal life. Their mere presence represents the artist's resilience in the face of tragedy. In *The Mother* especially, Käthe had confronted her personal grief and had gone beyond it: the work both grieves the loss of life and protests the forces that caused it. In *The Mother* and *The Father* she addresses all who are victims of the tyranny of war, comforting them and herself with all the love she can summon.

According to her friend and colleague Otto Nagel, the sculptures were "the artistic sensation of the day"[72] and established Kollwitz as a great sculptor as well. How happy she was! "I have once more," she wrote, "had that glorious feeling of happiness, that happiness which cannot be compared with anything else, which springs from being able to cope with one's work."[73]

The sculptures had still to be converted to granite, a labor that required an additional year. Before their transportation to Belgium, they were exhibited at the old National Gallery. Kollwitz had been anxious about finding a safe location for this exhibit, a place not yet "taken over by the Right,"[74] fearing that unless the figures were properly guarded, they "might be scrawled over with swastikas." After a display of two weeks at the National Gallery, "the public has shown such great interest that the exhibition has been extended for another week."[75]

Through protracted and difficult negotiations with the German Republic, the German national railway, the Belgian government, and the Brussels cemetery board, expense-free shipment of the sculptures was at last arranged. Käthe and Karl went to Roggevelde in order to direct their placement. On arrival, Käthe's first impression was that there was something strange about the cemetery.

> It has been leveled. And it seems smaller because the unknown soldiers have all been buried in pairs. Now it has been turned into a regular rectangle. The small tin crosses have been replaced by somewhat larger wooden crosses. The rows run with perfect regu-

larity, but the space between the crosses is not always equal. . . . Now the cemetery seems more monotonous than it did. Only three crosses are planted with roses. On Peter's grave they are in bloom, red ones. . . . The space in front, which has been reserved for the figures, is smaller than I thought. It too is in lawn. . . .

The British and Belgian cemeteries seem brighter, in a certain sense more cheerful and cosy, more familiar than the German cemeteries. I prefer the German ones. The war was not a pleasant affair; it isn't seemly to prettify with flowers the mass deaths of all these young men. A war cemetery ought to be somber.[76]

Large stone pedestals had been cut and were placed side by side, a few feet apart, at the head of the cemetery. With two other men and Karl, Käthe discussed the distance separating the sculptures until, finally, after thorough consideration, the space between the parent figures was agreed upon. With dollies, pulleys, and lifts, workmen moved *The Mother* painstakingly into place. Once it was set on the pedestal, however, it leaned too far forward because of the sloping terrain. The figure had to be removed and the pedestal adjusted so that the statue would be slightly raised.

The placement of *The Father* was extremely difficult. Käthe had planned that the figure should gaze out over the entire cemetery. Instead—again because of the rolling terrain— it appeared to be "staring down, brooding."[77] This spatial and stylistic alteration frustrated her; but it was mechanically impossible to alter the position of the figure. Although Karl assured her that the appearance of both sculptures was impressive, she felt depressed at the outcome.

The next afternoon, before they returned to Berlin, Karl and Käthe visited Roggevelde for the last time. Morning rain had made the new lawn spongy and mosslike. Käthe walked to the end of the cemetery and turned around to look at her granite sculptures at the distant entrance, and the mood of yesterday left her. The figures did cast a living spell of love in grief. Yes, they spoke. And breathed a life of their own. They were the solemn gatekeepers, the bereaved guardians of the young men before them. The sculpted parents were one with the still crosses, in silent communion.

She walked slowly toward Peter's grave, remembering her eighteen years with him, the same number of years trying to awaken his presence in the clay. At his grave she stopped and stood a long time, staring at its wet, green grass and the red roses twined around its cross. Then she looked up at her own granite face, bowed low in mourning, her kneeling, draped body a flow of tears.

> I stood before the woman, looked at her—my own face—and I wept and stroked her cheeks. Karl stood close behind me—I did not even realize it. I heard him whisper, "Yes, yes." How close we were to one another then![78]

## NOTES

1 Kollwitz, *Diary and Letters*, p. 64, entry of April 27, 1915. "I am working on the offering. I had to—it was an absolute compulsion—change everything. The figure bent under my hands of itself, as if obeying its own will—bent over forward. Now it is no longer the erect woman it had been. She bows far forward and holds out her child in deepest humility." I have taken the liberty of placing the 1915 experience in this chapter, which begins in 1920. Although the specific work described in the 1915 journal entry cannot be identified with certainty, what is significant about the transformation is that Kollwitz followed its lead, and that the changed pose is very similar to the final one of *The Mother* of Peter's memorial, a work with which she was actively engaged in 1920.

2 *Ibid.*, p. 97.

3 *Ibid.*, pp. 97–98.

4 Kollwitz, *Tagebuchblätter und Briefe*, ed. Hans Kollwitz (Berlin: Gebrüder Mann Verlag, 1948), p. 87.

5 Letter from Mrs. Fritz Kortner (niece of the artist) to Mr. Erich Cohn, dated March, 1946. Courtesy of Carl Zigrosser, Carl Zigrosser Manuscript Files, Rare Book Collection, University of Pennsylvania Library, Philadelphia, Pa.

6 Kollwitz, *Diary and Letters*, p. 98.

7 Nagel, *Käthe Kollwitz*, p. 47.
8 Kollwitz, *Diary and Letters*, p. 96.
9 Smedley, "Germany's Artist of the Masses," p. 9.
10 Kollwitz, *Diary and Letters*, p. 96.
11 Kollwitz, *Tagebuchblätter und Briefe*, p. 86.
12 Kollwitz, *Diary and Letters*, pp. 98–99.
13 *Ibid.*, p. 73.
14 *Ibid.*, pp. 17–18.
15 *Ibid.*, pp. 161–162.
16 *Ibid.*, p. 96.
17 *Ibid.*, p. 100.
18 *Ibid.*, pp. 103–104.
19 Bonus-Jeep, *Sechzig Jahre*, p. 217.
20 Kollwitz, *Tagebuchblätter und Briefe*, p. 86.
21 Kollwitz, *Diary and Letters*, p. 85.
22 *Ibid.*
23 *Ibid.*, pp. 86–87.
24 *Ibid.*, p. 104.
25 Kollwitz, *Briefe der Freundschaft*, p. 95.
26 Bonus-Jeep, *Sechzig Jahre*, p. 176.
27 Kollwitz, *Diary and Letters*, p. 104.
28 In the Peace Collection, Swarthmore College Library, Swarthmore, Pennsylvania
29 John Lauritsen and David Thorstad, *The Early Homosexual Rights Movement (1864–1935)* (New York: Times Change Press, 1974), pp. 11, 14.
30 Kollwitz, *Tagebuchblätter und Briefe*, pp. 96–97.
31 Kollwitz, *Diary and Letters*, p. 93.
32 *Ibid.*, p. 101.
33 Bonus-Jeep, *Sechzig Jahre*, p. 134.
34 *Ibid.*
35 This first print is in the private collection of Margaret Gaughan Klitzke.
36 Kollwitz, *Diary and Letters*, p. 8.
37 *Ibid.*, p. 157.
38 Kollwitz, *Tagebuchblätter und Briefe*, p. 87.
39 Nagel, *Käthe Kollwitz*, p. 48.
40 Mrs. Fritz Kortner to Erich Cohn, March, 1946.
41 Agnes Smedley, "Germany's Artist of the Masses," pp. 8–9.
42 Mrs. Fritz Kortner to Erich Cohn, March, 1946.
43 Agnes Smedley, "Germany's Artist of the Masses," pp. 8–9.
44 Bonus-Jeep, *Sechzig Jahre*, p. 63.
45 Mrs. Fritz Kortner to Erich Cohn, March, 1946.
46 Kollwitz, *Diary and Letters*, p. 112.
47 *Ibid.*, p. 108.
48 *Ibid.*, pp. 108–109.
49 Kollwitz, *Tagebuchblätter und Briefe*, p. 76.
50 Kollwitz, *Diary and Letters*, p. 101.
51 Kollwitz, *Tagebuchblätter und Briefe*, p. 76.
52 Nagel, *Käthe Kollwitz*, p. 52.
53 Six of the *Secreta* drawings were reproduced for the first time in Otto Nagel, *The Drawings of Käthe Kollwitz*, nos. 559–63, p. 299.

54 Kollwitz, *Diary and Letters*, p. 111.

55 Bonus-Jeep, *Sechzig Jahre*, p. 217.

56 Kollwitz, *Diary and Letters*, pp. 165-166.

57 *Ibid.*, p. 166.

58 Bonus-Jeep, *Sechzig Jahre*, p. 203.

59 Faith Ringgold, "The Gedok Show and the Lady Left," *Feminist Art Journal*, Fall 1972, p. 8.

60 Kollwitz, *Diary and Letters*, p. 79.

61 *Ibid.*, p. 142.

62 *Ibid.*, p. 97.

63 *Ibid.*

64 *Selbstbildnis, en face, lachend*, approximately 1888/89 as given in Nagel, *The Drawings of Käthe Kollwitz*, no. 7, p. 177.

65 Kollwitz, *Diary and Letters*, p. 114.

66 *Arbeiters International Zeitung* (no. 20, 1927) as found in Otto Nagel, *Käthe Kollwitz*, p. 260.

67 Carl Zigrosser, *Prints and Drawings of Käthe Kollwitz* (New York: Dover Publications, Inc., 1969), p. vii.

68 Kollwitz, *Diary and Letters*, p. 115.

69 *Ibid.*, p. 102.

70 *Ibid.*, p. 115.

71 *Ibid.*, p. 119.

72 Nagel, *Käthe Kollwitz*, p. 64.

73 Kollwitz, *Diary and Letters*, p. 120.

74 *Ibid.*

75 Nagel, *Käthe Kollwitz*, p. 69.

76 Kollwitz, *Diary and Letters*, pp. 121-122.

77 *Ibid.*, p. 122.

78 *Ibid.*

# 8

## Some day
## a new ideal will arise.

*They were strolling* side by side along the shore of the crystal mountain lake, shaded slightly by the gnarled, delicate branches of olive trees. The path wound around the lake, near the sound of the waves, now swelling, now sighing, in their rush toward the white, water-smoothed stones on the shore.

Käthe and Karl watched passing sails shimmer yellow-white against the dazzling blue of lake and sky. Käthe looked at the mountain rising from the opposite shore, thinking how wonderful it would be to climb, grabbing branches and roots for leverage, pulling herself up on vines, drinking from cool, clear streams, then relishing the view below from the highest peak.

She turned to Karl, knowing that he felt the same longing but that such a climb was equally impossible for him. Walking was still their favorite pastime, but at sixty-five and sixty-nine, Käthe and Karl were learning to accept lessened physical exertion. She was thankful that they were together in their old age.[1]

Their southern vacation was soon over; it was the last relatively carefree trip they were to enjoy. By April, 1933, Berlin was under Nazi rule: Adolf Hitler had established a dictatorship.

At the beginning of 1933, President von Hindenburg, backed by German industrialists, the military, and the aristocracy, had appointed Hitler to the chancellorship. Not satisfied with anything short of a dictatorship, Hitler called for parliamentary elections to be held March 5. The Nazis made use of Hitler's new, official powers, in the pre-election period, to step up the chaos and terror they had already set in motion—surprise house searches and arrests, general and specific intimidation and threats, the imprisonment of Jews, Communists, pacifists, homosexuals. In the elections, seventeen million Germans (forty-four percent of the electorate) voted for the National Socialist party, a victory that, combined with the vote for the allied right-wing Nationalist party, gave Hitler fifty-two percent of the Reichstag seats. When, on March 23, Hitler demanded dictatorial powers from the Reichstag, the only dissenting votes were those of the Social Democrats. The Communist representatives had not been seated, the Nazis having declared the Communist vote illegal—an illegal act itself, but one that went unchallenged. The power of Adolf Hitler and his National Socialist German Workers' Party was absolute.

The coup affected Kollwitz immediately. Along with other outstanding progressives who feared a Nazi takeover, she and her husband had signed a public manifesto calling for unity among the disintegrating Left in the March 5 elections. It was a courageous but futile try, for the appeal was issued only a few days before the Nazis' burning of the Reichstag building and the ensuing consolidation of Hitler's power. The Nazis threatened to break up the Academy unless Kollwitz and her colleague, writer Heinrich Mann, a cosigner of the petition, both resigned.

> Dear Jeep! Has the Academy affair reached your ears yet? That Heinrich Mann and I, because we signed the manifesto calling for unity of the parties of the left, must leave the Academy. It was all terribly unpleasant for the Academy directors. For fourteen years (the same fourteen that Hitler has branded the "evil years") I have worked together peacefully with these people. Now the Academy directors have had to ask me to resign. Otherwise the Nazis had threatened to break up the Academy. Naturally I complied. So did Heinrich Mann. Municipal Architect Wagner also resigned, in sympathy

with us. —But they are allowing me to keep my position until October 1, along with my full salary and the rooms I use. I am greatly relieved about this, because I have a largish group in clay over there and would have had no place to put it if they had evicted me straight off. . . .[2]

In *Die Frau* ("Woman"), the magazine supporting the women's movement with the largest distribution, writers had pointed out the danger in store for women in general and feminists in particular if the Nazis gained power. The Nazi romanticization of motherhood was rightly perceived by feminists as an insidious disguise for misogyny. A woman representative in the Reichstag reported that at one point, when a Social Democrat representative was lamenting the loss of her son in World War I, a brown-shirted Nazi shouted, "For that you she-goats were made!"[3]

In 1928 the women's movement had helped to block the Nazi rise to power. In order to defeat the formidable coalition presented by the SPD, middle-road and moderate-left parties, and the women's movement, the Nazis used simple but effective psychological weapons. While carefully cultivating the loyalty, love, and dedication of those out of power, they proceeded, at the same time, to brand those in power as disloyal to National Socialism, hence, disloyal to Germany.

From the outset, the Nazis directed different appeals to males and females. For men and boys, love of state and the common interests of the nation were paramount, preceding individual concerns; comradeship was sacred, and the virtues of hard work, perseverance, thrift, loyalty, hardihood, and military courage were extolled. In every mess hall the militaristic motto of "Live truly, fight bravely, and die laughing!" was displayed prominently in large letters. As in World War I, sacrifice of one's life for the state was considered the highest good. In contrast, propaganda aimed at women and girls appealed to more private emotions: love of heroes, children, God, and the leader were glorified. Love for Hitler—*Der Führer* ("The Leader")—and for his army of brown-shirted storm troopers was exalted. Above all, women were made to feel important not just as mothers and wives, but as Mothers of German children and German wives.

This romantic propaganda appealed to thousands of women, young and old, whose family life had been disrupted during the war and postwar years; many yearned for the stability of fathers, husbands, and sons. Hitler, a bachelor who proclaimed himself a celibate, provided women with a fantasy father: belonging to no one, he could belong to all.

In spite of the influence of feminism during the preceding period, women responded positively to these irrational appeals. Meanwhile, the numerous organizations of the women's movement were infiltrated and subverted, their members indoctrinated in the chauvinist, militaristic ideology of National Socialism. Leading feminists in politics were attacked as Marxists, as enemies of the state and the family, as murderers because of their proabortion stands. Kollwitz was not the only one to be removed from her job and replaced by a male Nazi; her fate was shared by women eminent in many fields, and by all feminists prominent in politics. Less than five years after it had begun, GEDOK was closed down by the Nazis and abandoned by its members. The Women's Bureau—part of the Office of the Interior—was closed, and Gertrud Bäumer, its administrator, forced to resign. She was replaced by a man who aroused so much hostility, even among Nazi women, that he was promptly supplanted by a woman, Gertrud Scholtz-Klink. True to her title, *Die Führerin*, she was a female blueprint of the misogynous *Führer.*

Now the fourteen short years of feminist public influence came to a close. This demise coincided with the decline of Kollwitz' prominence as an artist. She was still appreciated by the working class and, in the wake of repression, by a diminishing circle of artists and devotées. But by the fall of 1933, her wide and profound influence as an artist and independent socialist had waned. She had publicly opposed National Socialism and accepted the consequence of official condemnation with characteristic stoicism.

> I want to and must be among those who have been slapped down. The financial loss you mention follows as a matter of course. Thousands are going through the same experience. It is nothing to complain about.[4]

For a while, Kollwitz' work was still occasionally displayed. She was among the artists represented in the 1933 all-sculpture Academy show. However, at the last moment before the opening, with no explanation, two of her pieces were removed, along with three works by Barlach.[5]

She had suffered governmental derogation on earlier occasions, but never outright censorship. The Nazi regime denied Kollwitz the avenue to the public that every artist, no matter how introspective, needs in order to create. Independent though she was, she had always sought simplified and, sometimes, immediate communication through her work. In spite of her many years of membership in the Secession (which had now been forced to disband), Kollwitz, unlike many of her male colleagues, had never really benefited from the intercommunication of a "clique" or "school"; this was in part due to her artistic independence, in part due to the social inaccessibility of these male-oriented groups, and also due to Kollwitz' shyness. Exhibits had marked the few occasions in her career in which Käthe had been able to share the expression of her most intimate self with other artists and the public. She had always been interested in responses to her work, and it was also noticeable, from the 1917 retrospective on, that a working pattern had developed in which she often experienced a joyfully productive period shortly after a showing. While she bowed to the inevitability of the changed conditions, given her unwillingness to bow to Nazi dicta on art, she did not pretend that she welcomed artistic isolation.

> Participation is good and vital, and it is sad to be excluded. For one is after all a leaf on the twig and the twig belongs to the whole tree. When the tree sways back and forth, the leaf is content to sway with it.[6]

A few of her pieces could still be found at the Crown Prince Palace until, in 1936, the Nazis ordered this museum closed to the public. She never again saw any of her work on public display.

Kollwitz moved from her Academy studio on Hardenburgstrasse to a large building on Klosterstrasse that housed many suites of artists and their studios. But between her ejection from the Academy studio and her relocation in the new studio, she was unable to continue with her sculpture, not having the space at home to work on it. Therefore, in the summer of 1934, she returned to an earlier plan to do a series on the theme of death. She was not sanguine about its value, as she worked.

> The work I am doing does not satisfy me at all. "It's all been done before." When I worked it out for the first time it may have been no better, but it was more necessary for me. That is after all the crux of the matter.

> I thought that now that I am really old I might be able to handle this theme in a way that would plumb depths. . . . But that is not the case. . . . At the very point when death becomes visible behind everything, it disrupts the imaginative process. . . .

> I start off indecisively, soon tire, need frequent pauses and must turn for counsel to my own earlier works.[7]

Regardless of these defeated, negative comments, Kollwitz' powers did not fail her in the eight profoundly moving lithographs of the cycle *Tod* [Death]. Lise once said that her sister had carried on a dialogue with death all her life;[8] in this last great series, the artist interpreted eight different "conversations" and subsequent revelations on the theme.

The dramatic flying cape, the black lines of Death's wiry, long arms in *Tod greift in Kinderschar* [Death Swoops Upon a Group of Children] are breathtaking. In this print, as in *Frau reicht dem Tod die Hand* [Woman Entrusts Herself to Death], *Tod hält Mädchen im Schoss* [Death with Girl in Lap] and *Tod packt eine Frau* [Death Clutches a Woman], Kollwitz' consummate skill and insight are evident in each forceful line, each apt image. In *Death Clutches a Woman*, the repeating lines and movement of Death, the woman, and the child she grasps to her breasts, create a compelling effect, as much as does the awed horror on the woman's face. In the print *Tod wird als Freund erkannt* [Death Recognized as a Friend] and in the final *Ruf des Todes* [The Call of Death], we see the artist herself. Kollwitz appears sometimes to be more man than woman, sometimes more woman than man—but above all, a person whose aging has formed undifferentiated body characteristics. In the eight lithographs of *Death*, the artist's consciousness transcends her ego. Throughout, her vision is as inexorable as death itself.

Within a year Kollwitz poured out these eight plates—as well as her well-known, close-up self-portrait of 1934—as if they were effortless. In fact, the opposite was true, for now, as always, she subscribed to the principle that "one can allow oneself emotional outpourings only after strenuous intellectual labors."[9] The enormous discipline she had developed had enabled her to view death with objectivity. She had even been able to deal with Konrad's death, in 1932, in subsequent penetrating studies. Through years of careful preparatory work, at least fourteen other graphics, not including prints within the four major cycles, and countless drawings, she had hewed, honed, and distilled her feelings to a final essence in *Death*.

On July 13, 1936, Lina answered a heavy knock at the door. Two officers of the Gestapo stood in the hall. They were looking for Frau Kollwitz: Was she at home?

At the sight of old Lina's face, Kollwitz knew that the Gestapo had come. She could scarcely be astounded. Neither she, nor her family, nor various friends were in good political repute; both Karl and Hans had been, for a time, barred by the Nazis from practicing; Liebermann, an old colleague from The Secession, had been forbidden to paint and had died physically and spiritually broken. Many Jews, Communists, artists, and intellectuals she knew had suffered even worse persecution.

She went to meet the men with her usual quiet dignity. Their questions were about a recent article—part of which was an interview with her—that had appeared in *Izvestia*, the popular Soviet periodical.

Not long before, Kollwitz and her old friend Otto Nagel had been interviewed by a foreign journalist. While they had responded to the writer's sympathy with them as artists and antifascists, they had thought that they were being reasonably careful of what they had said. They had evidently not been careful enough.

Kollwitz' name had appeared in the article, but Nagel's had not. The Gestapo officers interrogated her for some time. They were interested in learning the identity of the unnamed German artist; they also wanted a retraction of Kollwitz' statements. They made it clear to her that if she did not cooperate with them, she would be imprisoned in a concentration camp; she must not expect that her age or her former reputation would protect her.[10]

Kollwitz remained silent. She was determined that nothing would wring Otto Nagel's name from her.

The following day, the Gestapo called again, this time in the person of a single representative. He found Kollwitz working in the ordered chaos of her studio, surrounded by her clay models of mothers and children, busts of herself, old bathtubs and garbage cans filled with clay or water. He examined the studio and her work, lifting aside the damp drop cloths to peer at unfinished sculptures. Having completed the inspection, he returned to the subject of the previous day: she must cooperate or face the inevitable consequences. Kollwitz then agreed to write a statement retracting the comments quoted in *Izvestia*. She would not agree, however, to divulge the identity of her fellow-artist.[11]

Neither she nor Karl expected the matter to end there. They spent the following day in a torment of fear and uncertainty, discussing the probabilities of arrest and imprisonment, and considering various alternative solutions—all of them unacceptable.[12]

Days of agitation went by; then months; then a year had passed. Although her work was ridiculed and reviled, Kollwitz was never again threatened personally. Lise and Jeep believed that her safety was provided by the neighborhood, in which she and Karl were longtime loved and respected residents. Whether or not the explanation lies there, Käthe and Karl had not expected to be safe; and on the day following the interrogation, they had arrived at a mutual "solution." Each thereafter carried a vial of poison, in case of being taken into the custody of the Nazis at some future time.[13]

Except for one large sculpture, *Gruppe* [The Group], Kollwitz now worked exclusively on small sculptures. Her eyes and body were growing weak, and furthermore, she did not have enough money to buy the materials required for large sculptures.

In 1936 she finished *The Group* and had it cast in cement—the cheapest and most durable cast she could afford. A sensuous portrait of a mother and two tiny children, *The Group* now marks the spot where she lived for so many years. It stands today in a small commemorative park, Käthe Kollwitz Platz, on Käthe Kollwitzstrasse in East Berlin. On her seventieth birthday she dedicated *The Group* to Ottilie—also a graphic artist, excelling in woodcuts. She wrote her daughter-in-law:

> For some time I have had the idea of giving you a very good reproduction of the group, and inscribing it: "The Mother—to the Mother—from the Mother." For there is a close tie between you and me and the work itself. I was working on this theme even before the war. Then everything else intervened. When I transferred from Siegmundshof [her first sculpture studio] to the Academy, I had a mold made and the piece cast along with the work for the soldiers' cemetery. But the piece had to be totally changed. For in the meantime the twins had come into the world, and ever since seeing you with a child in each arm I knew that I had to extend the work and have a child in it. And so the whole grew slowly until now, when it is finished at last. Now you know how intimately you are a part of it.—You Mother![14]

Käthe celebrated her seventieth birthday at Reinerz with Karl, Lise, and Lise's daughter, Katta—a professional dancer who, since 1933, had been forbidden to perform with her international troupe. Katta, for the occasion, "had put on that beautiful long silk dress with the big flowers and the famous lowcut back."[15] After a dinner of soup, trout, roast chicken and champagne, Lise treated Käthe to a rare automobile drive through the mountains. Käthe delighted in the drive, the laughter, the singing to the tune of Katta's lively accordion. In the evening, there was a birthday cake with seventy candles.

On that birthday she received more than one hundred and fifty letters and telegrams from all over the world. These expressions of affection and appreciation cheered her tremendously: "I am very happy about the deep and wide response my life work has had in Germany, and outside of Germany also. God knows I can be happy about that."[16]

With fresh energy, Kollwitz worked on three small, powerful sculptures: a non-religious pietà, a group called *Turm der Mütter* [Tower of Mothers], similar in tone and form to the woodcut *The Mothers*, and a self-portrait bust.

By the following year, 1938, she had finished *Tower of Mothers*. Local artists on Klosterstrasse were organizing an exhibit, and she entered this small piece. The women in this work, like those in the woodcut *The Mothers*, militantly defend their children from sacrifice in war.

The Nazis removed this small sculpture from the obscure show. Kollwitz' art had long since been officially labeled "degenerate," so the removal of the piece was not a surprise. Nor was it a surprise that there was no protest. The "silence" Käthe had remarked in connection with the expulsion of her work from a 1936 Academy show was now complete. At that time she had written:

> There is this curious silence surrounding the expulsion of my work from the Academy show. . . . Scarcely anyone had anything to say to me about it. I thought people would come, or at least write— but no. Such a silence all around us.[17]

Under the weight of agonizing political conditions, artistic isolation, and her advancing years, she had begun to absorb the silence into herself. "One turns more and more to silence. All is still. I sit in Mother's chair by the stove, evenings, when I am alone."[18]

On October 24, 1938, Barlach died. Kollwitz had respected no other artist so much. He had inspired her to try woodcuts, and was, in her opinion, the one contemporary who had shared her aims and had successfully achieved them. His death moved Kollwitz to execute the very tender bronze relief *Klage* [Lament], a close-up of her face, half-covered and comforted by her hands. It was a sublime tribute to her former colleague and sometime mentor.

Relief required skills in composition and sculpture, both of which Kollwitz had highly developed. Having found this new medium through *Lament*, she now made numerous gravestone reliefs, on commission. She began a headstone relief for Karl and herself, entitling it *Rest in the Peace of His Hands* from a verse of Goethe. One of the most beautiful gravestone reliefs she designed was for a family called Levy—not among the thousands of Jews who had already fled Germany. In December, 1938, Kollwitz wrote:

> Dear Frau Levy! . . . I have been thinking continually about you, dear Frau Levy. Not only do my thoughts turn to the grave relief, but also to you. Believe me, we are all suffering the same and deeply. We feel pain and shame. And anger.
>
> What do you think you will do now? What will become of your children?[19]

The Nazis had finally banned Karl's practice altogether; the little income Käthe earned by commissions was helpful, although the two remained quite poor. A private collector purchased some of her sculptures. The collector, an American, had offered her refuge in the United States, but she had declined; she did not want to be separated from her family.[20]

In a journal entry of September 1938, she expressed her thankfulness that "war has been averted" by Chamberlain, and her fervent agreement with a British Member of Parliament that "there is nothing in this world important enough to justify unleashing another world war." She added: "God knows, not Deutschland, Deutschland *ueber* alles!"[21]

Her sentiments were not shared. At dawn on September 1, 1939, Hitler made the military move for which he had been preparing Germany. The most aggressive military power in the world, Germany had in 1938 annexed Austria, with its six-and-a-half million population, to the Third *Reich*, and had recently taken Czechoslovakia; now Hitler launched an attack on Poland by land, sea, and air. France and Great Britain, thus notified that the earlier "nonaggression" pact was null, declared war on Germany two days later. World War II had begun.

Karl Kollwitz had not been really well since the time of an unsuccessful eye operation for cataracts in the early 1930s. In 1939 he rallied from what appeared to be the end; but by the spring of 1940 he had become completely bedridden. Käthe wrote: "I am working on the small group in which the man—Karl—frees himself from me and withdraws from my arms."[22] While she tried to prepare herself for this withdrawal, it was not an easy matter.

Some years earlier, she had upbraided herself for the "half-truths" her journals presented about her relationship with Karl.

> Recently I began reading my old diaries. . . . I wrote nothing when Karl and I. . . . made each other happy; but long pages when we did not harmonize. As I read I distinctly felt what a half-truth a diary presents. . . . Karl was always at my side. And that is a happiness that I have fully realized only in these last years—that he and I are together. . . . He is no longer the same man he once was, and I am no longer the same woman. He has left many things behind him, has grown out of and above them. What has remained is his "innocence." . . . He has a really innocent heart, and from that comes his wonderful inward joyousness.[23]

Käthe was now Karl's constant nurse and companion, watching over him, arranging small pleasures, reading and reciting poems to him. In mid-July, she recorded very simply: "Karl has died, July 19, 1940."

From that day Käthe used a cane to help her walk.[24]

Kollwitz moved her studio from Klosterstrasse to her living room. Her small clay figures, wrapped in wet cloths, her sketchpads, portfolios, drawing easel, and cans of clay now stood alongside her bed, her desk, the old round dining table, and the living room couch and chairs. She could not afford to heat the entire apartment; she lived and worked beside the central wood heater.

That winter brought hardships. Fortunately, Lina and Klara, Lise's niece, were living with her, cooked for her, and helped her to get about. But without Karl she was terribly lonely; and the suffering caused by the war deeply disturbed her. Her own grandson Peter (her son Peter's namesake) had now joined the army. Work proceeded in fits and starts and subject to her waning physical strength; sometimes she worked for days at a time, then stopped for months. Irrevocably, she was old and infirm.

> It is of course bitter to experience it. The old Michelangelo drew a picture of himself in a kiddie car, and [Franz] Grillparzer says: "Once I was a poet, now I am none; the head on my shoulders is no longer mine." But that is simply the way things are.
>
> Yes, I must still say as I always have, that when a certain measure of suffering has been reached, man has the right to cut his life short. I am still far from that measure of suffering, in a physical or spiritual sense. And I also feel a timidity and fear of bringing death upon myself. I am afraid of dying—but being dead, oh yes, that to me is an appealing prospect. If it were only not for the necessity of parting from the few who are dear to me here.[25]

In January, 1942, Kollwitz produced her last graphic. In this lithograph she fiercely resisted the bombing, mass slaughter and sieges that were ravaging Europe. Her last testament to the world, appropriately, was a visualization of the creed she had come to live by. At age seventy-four she executed *Saatfrüchte sollen nicht vermahlen werden* [Seed for the planting must not be ground].

> I have finished my lithograph "Seed for the planting must not be ground." This time the seed for the planting—sixteen-year-old boys—are all around the mother, looking out from under her coat and wanting to break loose. But the old mother who is holding them together says, No! You stay here! For the time being you may play rough-and-tumble with one another. But when you are grown up you must get ready for life, not for war again.[26]

The work was her final presentation of the themes that had preoccupied her as an artist and as a person through the greatest portion of her working life.

(text continued on page 221)

Courtesy of Max Jacoby

PLATE 30. *Selbstbildnis, en face*
[Self-portrait bust] , 1937,
bronze sculpture.

PLATE 31. *Turm der Mütter*
[Tower of Mothers] , 1938,
bronze sculpture.

*219*

RNTE SEHEN, WAS K
RNTE FÜHLEN WAS W

PLATE 32. *Levy Grabrelief* [Grave Relief for the Levy Family], 1936–40, stone.

> The process is after all like the development of a
> piece of music. The fugues come back and inter-
> weave again and again. A theme may seem to have
> been put aside, but it keeps returning—the same
> thing in a somewhat changed and modulated form,
> and usually richer.[27]

The prohuman, antiwar lithograph was produced as
English and American bombing raids began to force thousands
of Berliners underground daily. It was difficult for Käthe and
her family to get to safety during the raids; with the aid of
Lina and Klara, Käthe was helped down three flights of stairs
to the cellar.

But the war had far worse torments in store for her. On
October 14, 1942, Hans brought word that Peter had fallen
in Russia.[28] Käthe and Karl had especially loved this first
grandchild, named after their own son. It was a terrible,
wrenching irony that their grandson's fate should have been
the same as that of his namesake. "Even then," Hans remembered, "she bore herself proudly, did not grieve openly, scarcely
wept; she tried to give us strength to bear it. But the blow had
been deep and damaging."[29]

In 1943 the artist created her last self-portrait, a charcoal
drawing. A very old person who, like the Kollwitz in the *Death*
cycle, appears no more female than male, sits passively before
us. She reflects upon, and accepts, the forces of time. Her
steady, direct gaze is familiar, but it is fixed upon a sight
beyond us: her wizened eyes see her age, her past, and imminent death.

This portrait, like the many preceding it, shows Kollwitz'
amazing ability to reveal herself through scrupulous, realistic
rendering of "the essentials." It is the last of eighty-four
self-portraits, possibly the longest chronology of self-portraits
by a woman in Western art, certainly a stunning psychological
charting of a woman's life.

By 1943 the bombing of Berlin had become severe. A
young sculptor, Margarete Böning, offered Käthe refuge at a
large country farmhouse in Nordhausen, southwest of Berlin,
where she was living with her children. Böning had admired
Kollwitz' work since the start of her own career. Käthe at
first refused, unwilling to fly from dangers that Lise, Katta,

*221*

and Klara had still to confront. Böning then generously insisted upon taking in all of the women.

In the summer of 1943, Käthe left Berlin. She said goodbye to "Aunt" Lina, who was returning to her rural home. With Lise, Katta, and Klara, Käthe traveled toward Nordhausen in a Red Cross truck. She was silent, remembering her half century in Berlin, so much of it that was dear spent within the tenement walls of her now-vacant home. She gazed at the passing meadows and farmlands, seeing none of it, her eyes blurred with tears.[30]

At Nordhausen, the stifling oppression of war-torn Berlin left her, and she felt rejuvenated. Margarete and her children were fun-loving extroverts, and their lively, often boisterous activity lifted her spirits. She sat in the garden and read—especially from her beloved Goethe—wrote letters, watched the young Bönings romp, or listened to them sing folksongs after dinner.[31] Margarete was very practical and capable, "a wonderful, charming woman,"[32] and Käthe was grateful to be in her home.

In her last years, Käthe was a prolific and affectionate letter writer, to relatively new friends as well as to Lise, Ottilie, Jeep, and Hans. In her correspondence she repeatedly expressed her gratitude for a long and fulfilling life. A loving letter to Georg Gretor, her foster son, is filled with nostalgia.

> Do you remember. . . . our theatricals! Schiller's *Love and Intrigue* and the *Lower Depths*—it went on forever. And the dogs Pitti and Anatol! When you sat around the oilcloth-covered table, each of you with a book in front of him, and Pitti would sit beside one of you, his head peering out from under one of your arms and resting gravely on the table beside the book! And how we worried about Pitti when he was picked up by the dogcatcher again and you went to bail him out. And how afraid I was when you two did not come home from Burg. You had missed the train. Woetherstrasse was quite dark, and I walked up and down it, terribly nervous, until at last I saw the two silhouettes, yours and Peter's.
>
> Oh, Georg, how good it all was. . . . the fullness and richness of our lives overwhelms me again and again

222

with feelings of gratitude. Let us tell you once more
how we all have loved you.[33]

Six months after she arrived at Nordhausen, on November
23, 1943, her three-floor tenement home in Berlin was destroyed by bombs, the building burned to the ground. Klara
and Hans had earlier made trips to bring as much of Kollwitz'
work as possible into safety, but even so, a sizable amount
was destroyed. Much of her work had already been deliberately
destroyed by the Nazis; her art was the victim both of repression and of war.

Family photographs, letters, mementos of Karl, of her
lost son, and her lost grandson were swept away, along with
the house. Yet even in this blow she saw some philosophic
gain.

> It was my home for more than fifty years. Five
> persons whom I have loved so dearly have gone
> away from those rooms forever. Memories filled
> all the rooms. . . . But there is also some good in
> the total annihilation of the past. Only an idea
> remains, and that is fixed in the heart.[34]

A week later bombs struck Hans' and Ottilie's home
in Lichtenrade, razing it. Now her children and grandchildren
were also homeless.

> Dear children! I hold Hans' letter in my hand, open
> it and find the news. Ah, yes, such is our life; our
> fates are so entangled with one another. What is
> left now? Love that grows firmer and firmer. You
> must go on living. I too want to go on living in
> order to see you again. At least once more. Oh God,
> life is hard. Keep up your courage! And Ottilie,
> keep your studio. Courage![35]

Every day the war intensified. Kollwitz grew, if possible,
more firm in the convictions that had begun to shape themselves during World War I.

> Every war already carries within it the war which
> will answer it. Every war is answered by a new war,
> until everything, everything is smashed. . . . That is
> why I am so wholeheartedly for a radical end to

this madness, and why my only hope is in a world socialism. You know what my conception of that is and what I consider the only possible prerequisites for it. Pacifism simply is not a matter of calm looking on; it is work, hard work.[36]

Now life at Nordhausen had become precarious. Aside from the dangers of air raids, food rations were pitifully reduced, and the house could no longer be heated.

Prince Ernst Heinrich of Saxony, a collector ardently appreciative of Kollwitz' contributions to art, heard of her plight. He offered her a suite of rooms at his estate in Moritzburg, near Dresden. At her family's urging, she accepted.

Lise, Katta, and Klara returned to Berlin. Hans' daughter, Jutta, came to care for her grandmother at Moritzburg in the autumn of 1944. By this time, Käthe had suffered heart failure and, for many months past, she had known an "unquenchable longing for death."[37] But, alternately, she was lively and even capable of a rare streak of humor.

> "Just think, I again dreamed that I had died, and you can't imagine how terribly boring it was. Do you know the poem of Heine's: 'And I'm afraid, yes I'm afraid the resurrection will not come off so easily'?"[38]

Jutta looked after her own and her grandmother's physical needs and the care of the two-room apartment—"working tremendously hard," Käthe observed in a letter to Lise.[39] In the evening, Jutta read to her grandmother, usually from Goethe, and the two women talked. Kollwitz reverted again and again to the war.

> "Do you see those lovely little apples out there? Everything could be so beautiful if it were not for this insanity of the war. . . .

> "But some day a new ideal will arise and there will be an end of all wars. . . . People will have to work hard for that new state of things, but they will achieve it."[40]

Käthe Kollwitz died affirming that faith on April 22, 1945, four months before the end of World War II. She died without worldly possessions, but rich in her own person. In her time she had developed the strength "to take life as it is and, unbroken by life—without complaining and overmuch weeping—to do one's work powerfully. Not to deny oneself, the personality one happens to be, but to embody it."[41]

## NOTES

1 Kollwitz, *Diary and Letters*, pp. 169–170, letter to Hans, headed "Malcesine, May 1931."

2 Bonus-Jeep, *Sechzig Jahre*, p. 263.

3 Clifford Kirkpatrick, *Nazi Germany: Its Women and Family Life* (New York: Bobbs-Merrill Co., Inc., 1938), p. 52.

4 Kollwitz, *Diary and Letters*, p. 171.

5 *Ibid.*

6 *Ibid.*

7 *Ibid.*, pp. 123–124.

8 *Ibid.*, p. 195.

9 *Ibid.*, p. 143.

10 Käthe Kollwitz, *"Ich will wirken,"* p. 117.

11 *Ibid.*, and Nagel, *Käthe Kollwitz*, p. 76.

12 Käthe Kollwitz, *"Ich will wirken,"* p. 117.

13 *Ibid.*

14 Kollwitz, *Diary and Letters*, p. 172.

15 *Ibid.*, p. 173.

16 *Ibid.*, p. 174.

17 *Ibid.*, p. 125.

18 *Ibid.*

19 Käthe Kollwitz, *Briefe der Freundschaft*, p. 86.

20 Käthe Kollwitz to Erich Cohn, October 1939, Courtesy of Carl Zigrosser. Carl Zigrosser Manuscript File, Rare Books Collection, University of Pennsylvania Library, Philadelphia, Pa.

21 Kollwitz, *Diary and Letters*, p. 125.

22 *Ibid.*, p. 127.

23 *Ibid.*, p. 111.

24 Nagel, *Käthe Kollwitz*, p. 80.

25 Kollwitz, *Diary and Letters*, pp. 129–130.

26 Bonus-Jeep, *Sechzig Jahre*, pp. 293–294.

27 Kollwitz, *Diary and Letters*, p. 141.

28 *Ibid.*, p. 9.

29 *Ibid.*

30 Bonus-Jeep, *Sechzig Jahre*, p. 295.

31 Kollwitz, *Diary and Letters*, p. 9.

32 *Ibid.*, p. 180.

33 *Ibid.*, pp. 179–180.

34 *Ibid.*, pp. 180–181.

35 *Ibid.*, p. 181.

36 *Ibid.*, pp. 183–184.

37 *Ibid.*, p. 187.

38 Jutta Kollwitz, "The Last Days of Kaethe Kollwitz," *ibid.*, p. 197.

39 Kollwitz, *Diary and Letters*, p. 191.

40 Jutta Kollwitz, "The Last Days," *ibid.*, p. 198.

41 *Ibid.*, p. 78.

# EPILOGUE
## Käthe Kollwitz

I

Held between wars
my lifetime
        among wars, the big hands of the world of death
my lifetime
listens to yours.

The faces of the sufferers
in the street, in dailiness,
their lives showing
through their bodies
a look as of music
the revolutionary look
that says   I am in the world
to change the world
my lifetime
is to love to endure to suffer the music
to set its portrait
up as a sheet of the world
the most moving the most alive
Easter and bone
and Faust walking among the flowers of the world
and the child alive within the living woman, music of man,
and death holding my lifetime between great hands
the hands of enduring life
that suffers the gifts and madness of full life, on earth, in our time,
and through my life, through my eyes, through my arms and hands
may give the face of this music in portrait waiting for
the unknown person
held in the two hands, you.

II

Woman as gates, saying:
"The process is after all like music,

like the development of a piece of music.
The fugues come back and
                              again and again
interweave.
A theme may seem to have been put aside,
but it keeps returning—
the same thing modulated,
somewhat changed in form.
Usually richer.
And it is very good that this is so."


A woman pouring her opposites.
"After all there are happy things in life too.
Why do you show only the dark side?"
"I could not answer this. But I know—
In the beginning my impulse to know
the working life
                  had little to do with
pity or sympathy.
                  I simply felt
that the life of the workers was beautiful."


She said, "I am groping in the dark."


She said, "When the door opens, of sensuality,
then you will understand it too. The struggle begins.
Never again to be free of it,
often you will feel it to be your enemy.
Sometimes
you will almost suffocate,
such joy it brings."


Saying of her husband: "My wish
is to die after Karl.
I know no person who can love as he can,
with his whole soul.
Often this love has oppressed me;
I wanted to be free.
But often too it has made me
so terribly happy."

She said: "We rowed over to Carrara at dawn,
climbed up to the marble quarries
and rowed back at night. The drops of water
fell like glittering stars
from our oars."

She said: "As a matter of fact,
I believe
       that bisexuality
in almost   a necessary factor
in artistic production; at any rate,
the tinge of masculinity within me
helped me
       in my work."

She said: "The only technique I can still manage.
It's hardly a technique at all, lithography.
In it
     only the essentials count."

A tight-lipped man in a restaurant last night
     saying to me:
"Kollwitz? She's too black-and-white."

### III

Held among wars, watching
    all of them
    all these people
    weavers,
    Carmagnole

Looking at
    all of them
    death, the children
    patients in waiting-rooms
    famine
    the street
    the corpse with the baby
    floating, on the dark river

A woman seeing
 the violent, inexorable
 movement of nakedness
 and the confession of No
 the confession of great weakness, war,
 all streaming to one son killed, Peter;
 even the son left living; repeated,
 the father, the mother; the grandson
 another Peter killed in another war; firestorm;
 dark, light, as two hands,
 this pole and that pole as the gates.

What would happen if one woman told the truth about her life?
The world would split open

IV SONG: THE CALLING-UP

Rumor, stir of ripeness
rising within this girl
sensual blossoming ·
of meaning, its light and form.

The birth-cry summoning
out of the male, the father
from the warm woman
a mother in response.

The word of death
calls up the fight with stone
wrestle with grief with time
from the material make
an art harder than bronze.

V SELF-PORTRAIT

Mouth looking directly at you
eyes in their inwardness looking
directly at you
half light half darkness
woman, strong, German, young artist

flows into
wide sensual mouth meditating
looking right at you
eyes shadowed with brave hand
looking deep at you
flows into
wounded brave mouth
grieving and hooded eyes
alive, German, in her first War
flows into
strength of the worn face
a skein of lines
broods, flows into
mothers among the war graves
bent over death
facing the father
stubborn upon the field
flows into
the marks of her knowing—
*Nie Wieder Krieg*
repeated in the eyes
flows into
"Seedcorn must not be ground"
and the grooved cheek
lips drawn fine
the down-drawn grief
face of our age
flows into
*Pieta*, mother and
between her knees
life as her son in death
pouring from the sky of
one more war
flows into
face almost obliterated
hand over the mouth forever
hand over one eye now
the other great eye
closed

*—Muriel Rukeyser* [1971]

# BIBLIOGRAPHY

## AUTOBIOGRAPHICAL

Kollwitz, Käthe. *Briefe der Freundschaft und Begegnungen* [Letters of Friendship and Acquaintance]. Edited by Hans Kollwitz. Munich: List Verlag, 1966. Handy chronology of letters.

——. *Ich sah die Welt mit liebevollen Blicken* [I Saw the World with Loving Eyes]. Hanover: Hans Kollwitz, 1970. Handsome edition; features family memorabilia.

——. *"Ich will wirken in dieser Zeit"* ["I Want to Exert Influence in this Time"]. Introduction by Friedrich Ahlers-Hestermann. Berlin: Gebrüder Mann Verlag, 1952. Convenient arrangement of diary entries and letters in one chronology. Most important source on Kollwitz' life in the Nazi era.

——. *Tagebuchblätter und Briefe* [Diary and Letters]. Edited by Hans Kollwitz. Berlin: Gebrüder Mann Verlag, 1948. Contains more intimate diary entries and letters than the English version.

——. *The Diary and Letters of Kaethe Kollwitz*. Edited by Hans Kollwitz. Translated by Richard and Clara Winston. Chicago: Henry Regnery Co., 1955. The English sourcebook on her life. Out of print.

West Berlin. Akademie der Künste. Tagebuchblätter [Diaries] 1909–1943 [by Käthe Kollwitz]. 11 vols. Handwritten in black or dark blue ink, on paper sized approximately 7 by 9 in.; her handwriting is quite readable as well as beautiful. *The* source on her life.

## LIFE AND WORKS

Bittner, Herbert. *Kaethe Kollwitz Drawings*. New York: Thomas Yoseloff Publishers, 1964. Excellent collection and reproduction of drawings; intelligent though sketchy introductory biography. Out of print.

Bonus-Jeep, Beate. *Sechzig Jahre Freudschaft mit Käthe Kollwitz* [Sixty Years of Friendship with Käthe Kollwitz]. Berlin: Boppard, Karl Rauch Verlag, 1948. Written by her best friend, Jeep; disorganized, but the most useful, intimate, woman-oriented text.

Devree, Howard. "Friend of Humanity." *New York Times Magazine* (November 18, 1945): 16–17. Devree, a widely published American critic, was a consistent admirer of Kollwitz, though he overstressed "mother love." Wrote many articles, with reproductions, in a deliberate effort to make her recognition "commensurate with her great gifts." He believed that "Käthe Kollwitz is one of the timeless."

Diel, Louise. *Käthe Kollwitz: ein Ruf ertönt, eine Einführung in das Lebenswerk der Künstlerin* [Käthe Kollwitz: The Call Resounded, an Introduction to the Life Work of the Artist]. Berlin: Furche-Kunstverein, 1927. Emphasizes compassionate motherhood. The book is hard to find in America.

Heilborn, Adolf. *Die Zeichner des Volks I: Käthe Kollwitz* [Draughtsmen of the People, I: Käthe Kollwitz]. Berlin: Rembrandt Verlag, 1929. Many good reproductions; text flowery but socialist, humanist oriented. Contains some valuable information.

———. *Käthe Kollwitz*. Frankfurt: Kunstverein, 1973. Excellent catalog of traveling exhibit of her work held from June, 1973, to February, 1974, at Frankfurt am Main, Stuttgart, and Berlin. Features cataloguing of German social, political, and economic history from 1871 to 1933, as well as an interesting article on how her work was interpreted by German critics, writers, and political organizations from 1893 to 1967.

———. *Käthe Kollwitz: Drawings, Etchings, Lithographs, Woodcuts, Sculpture*. Catalog 88, Israel Museum and Tel Aviv Museum. Jerusalem: 1972. Excellent compilation of biographical data with works.

———. *Käthe Kollwitz*. West Berlin: Akademie der Künste, 1967. Very good catalog of biographical material with drawings from the collection of Käthe-Kollwitz-Archiv, Akademie der Künste. The exhibit was held at the Academy in honor of the anniversary of her 100th year, from December 10, 1967, to January 7, 1968.

Klein, Mina C., and Klein, H. Arthur. *Käthe Kollwitz: Life in Art*. New York: Holt, Rinehart and Winston, 1972. Beautiful publication; excellent coverage of years 1933-1938.

Koerber, Lenka von. *Erlebtes mit Käthe Kollwitz* [Living with Käthe Kollwitz]. Berlin: Rutten and Loning, 1957. Duplicates much of Jeep's material; is not very intimate concerning Kollwitz, but describes more of the political and social atmosphere.

Lehrs, Max. "Käthe Kollwitz." *Zukunft* 5 (1901): 351-355. Lehrs was an established art critic, head of the Prints and Drawings Collection of the city museum of Dresden; from the beginning of Kollwitz' career he purchased her work.

Mansfield, Heinz. *Käthe Kollwitz: Bauernkreig*. Dresden: Verlag der Kunst, 1958. Socialist perspective, sensitive discussion of *The Peasant War*. A *Mappe*, or portfolio of loose reproductions, large size, on beige paper, beautifully reproduced.

McCausland, Elizabeth. *Käthe Kollwitz: Fifteen Lithographs*. New York: Curt Valentin and Henry C. Kleeman, 1941. First feminist-oriented critique of her work in English. As critic and feminist, McCausland appreciated Kollwitz fully: "Käthe Kollwitz at age seventy-four is a contemporary master. . . . Whenever her work is seen, it exerts an influence at once aesthetic and moral, creative and human, of an extent apparently incommensurate with the simple means the artist uses. . . . The subjection of women she recorded with stern realism was a deeper tragedy than can be righted with equal rights slogans. . . . " Unfortunately, apart from these two oversized pages, McCausland wrote little on Kollwitz.

Nagel, Otto. *Die Selbstbildnisse der Käthe Kollwitz* [The Self-portraits of Käthe Kollwitz]. Berlin: Henschelverlag, 1965. Beautiful, rare chronology of self-portraits. Introductory text.

———. *Käthe Kollwitz*. Old Greenwich, Conn.: New York Graphic Society, 1971. Good reproductions. Nagel was a friend of hers from 1920 on; during the Nazi period she protected him against persecution. Useful as a human document in some sections; point of view patriarchal.

———. *The Drawings of Käthe Kollwitz*. With the collaboration of Sibylle Schallenberg-Nagel and Hans Kollwitz. Edited by Werner Timm. New York: Crown Publications, Inc., 1972. Beautiful reproduction of some thirteen hundred (!) drawings, many of which have never been previously catalogued or published. The most important work on Kollwitz to date by an art historian; establishes Kollwitz as one of the world's great workers in the graphic arts. Timm is the first scholar to document her process of creativity by technical examination of drawings. Notable also for new biographical information. The price, $80.00, is outrageous but perhaps unavoidable due to the size of the book. The entire book is printed on glossy paper.

*Neue Sezession 1910 Katalog*. Berlin: Die Neue Sezession, 1910. Kollwitz was one of eight women artists listed in a roster of 228 including Manet, Klee, Picasso, etc.

Nundel, Harri. *Käthe Kollwitz*. Leipzig: VEB Bibliographischen Institut, 1964. Patriarchal point of view.

Smedley, Agnes. "Käthe Kollwitz: Germany's Artist of the Masses." *Industrial Pioneers* 2 (September, 1925): 8-13. Sympathetic interview by another independent socialist, feminist, and revolutionary.

Zigrosser, Carl. *The Prints and Drawings of Käthe Kollwitz*. New York: Dover Publications, Inc., 1969. Beautiful, large reproductions of her work at a reasonable price. Text informative but suffers from usual art history bias of sex and class. However, Zigrosser is to be thanked for bringing Kollwitz to the attention of many Americans with this inexpensive edition.

GENERAL

Barraclough, Geoffrey. *The Origins of Modern Germany*. New York: Capricorn Books, 1963.

Bebel, August. *Woman and Socialism*. Translated by Meta L. Stern. New York: Socialist Literature Co., 1910. Feminist, utopian; reveals sexist norms of the SPD.

Bridenthal, Renate. "Beyond Kinder, Küche, Kirche: Weimar Women at Work." *Central European History* 6 (June 1973): 148–166. Does not deal specifically with the women's movement but provides useful background to the changes that occurred in the women's movement during the 1920s.

Dawson, William Harbutt. *What is Wrong with Germany?* London: Longmans, Green, and Co., 1913.

Dolgoff, Sam. *Bakunin on Anarchy*. New York: Alfred A. Knopf, 1972. Erudite.

Frölich, Paul. *Rosa Luxemburg: Her Life and Work*. Newly translated by Johanna Hoornweg. New York: Monthly Review Press, 1972.

Hackett, Amy. "The German Women's Movement and Suffrage, 1890–1914: A Study of National Feminism." *Modern European Social History*. Edited by Robert J. Bezucha. Lexington, Mass.: Heath, 1972, pp. 354–386. Useful for background, especially in demonstrating that the German women's movement by no means began in the 1920s.

Harrison, John B., and Sullivan, Richard E. *A Short History of Western Civilization*. New York: Alfred A. Knopf, 1963. Adequate outline.

Holborn, Hajo. *A History of Modern Germany: 1840-1945*. New York: Alfred A. Knopf, Inc., 1969. Comprehensive.

Kirkpatrick, Clifford. *Nazi Germany: Its Women and Family Life*. New York: Bobbs-Merrill Co., 1938. The best feminist-oriented source of information on the subject I know of.

Klinger, Max. *Malerie und Zeichnung* [Painting and Drawing]. Berlin: Insel, 1891. Inselbucherie no. 263. Technical dissertation.

Lauritsen, John, and Thorstad, David. *The Early Homosexual Rights Movement (1864-1934)*. New York: Times Change Press, 1974. Informative documentation and feminist-oriented analysis of the first gay movement in Germany.

Luxemburg, Rosa. *Rosa Luxemburg Speaks*. Edited by Mary Alice Waters. New York: Pathfinder Press, 1970. Good historical background of Luxemburg's time.

Marx, Karl. *Capital and Other Writings*. New York: The Modern Library, Random House, Inc., 1959.

Puckett, Hugh. *Germany's Women Go Forward*. New York: Columbia

University Press, 1930. The best overall review of German women's rights movement in English for the period before 1930, although on individuals superceded by monographs written in the 1970s.

Nochlin, Linda. "Why Are There No Great Women Artists?" *Woman in Sexist Society*. Edited by Barbara K. Moran and Vivian Gornick. New York: Signet (New American Library), 1971, pp. 480-510. I disagree that there are no great women artists, but this article pioneered the way for a feminist examination of art institutions and the psychology of women artists.

Pevsner, Nicholas. *Academies of Art, Past and Present*. Cambridge: At the University Press, 1940. Feminist-oriented, valuable scholarly account of European institutions of art.

Raven, Arlene. "Woman's Art: A Theoretical Perspective." *Womanspace Journal* 1 (1973):1. Perceptive, pioneering discussion on the aesthetic and meaning of art by women.

Ringgold, Faith. "The Gedok Show and the Lady Left." *Feminist Art Journal*. Brooklyn, New York: FAJ, Inc., Fall 1972, p. 8. Whether she is writing, speaking, or creating, Ringgold's perceptions on women, art, and the women's movement always make good human and artistic sense. The *Feminist Art Journal* is an important new forum for and about women and art.

Rowbotham, Sheila. *Women, Resistance and Revolution: A History of Women and Revolution in the Modern World*. New York: Pantheon Books, 1972. A scholarly milestone on the subject; sensible feminist and Marxist analysis.

von Ossietsky, Carl. *The Stolen Republic: Selected Writings of Carl von Ossietsky*. Edited by Bruno Frei. Berlin: Seven Seas Publishers, 1971. Covers period before World War I through 1930. Excellent first-hand accounts and essays by a progressive journalist and publicist who was later imprisoned by the "Republic" (under the influence of the Nazis) for treason, and martyred by his imprisonment when the Nazis came to power. One of the best sources on this period.